LOCKHART BOGLE

First Published by
David Nutt in 1893

This facsimile edition has been carefully scanned
and reprinted in the traditional manner by
THE LOST LIBRARY
5 High Street,
Glastonbury UK BA6 9DP

The LOST LIBRARY is a publishing house based in
Glastonbury, UK, dedicated to the reproduction
of important rare esoteric and scholarly texts for
the discerning reader.

Cataloguing Information
The Secret Commonwealth
Kirk, Scott and Lang

ISBN 978 1 906621 31 5

Printed by Replika Press Pvt Ltd, India

THE LOST
LIBRARY

The Secret Commonwealth of

Elves, Fauns, & Fairies

A Study in Folk-Lore & Psychical Research. The
Text by Robert Kirk, M.A., Minister of
Aberfoyle, A.D. 1691. The Comment
by Andrew Lang, M.A.

A.D. 1893

PUBLISHED BY
THE LOST LIBRARY
GLASTONBURY, ENGLAND

Dedication.

TO

ROBERT LOUIS STEVENSON.

O Louis! you that like them maist,
Ye're far frae kelpie, wraith, and ghaist,
And fairy dames, no unco chaste,
    And haunted cell.
Among a heathen clan ye're placed,
    That kens na hell!

Ye hae nae heather, peat, nor birks,
Nae troot in a' your burnies lurks,
There are nae bonny U.P. kirks,
    An awfu' place!
Nane kens the Covenant o' Works
    Frae that of Grace!

But whiles, maybe, to them ye'll read
Blads o' the Covenanting creed,
And whiles their pagan wames ye'll feed
    On halesome parritch;
And syne ye'll gar them learn a screed
    O' the Shorter Carritch.

Yet thae uncovenanted shavers
Hae rowth, ye say, o' clash and clavers
O' gods and etins—auld wives' havers,
    But their delight;
The voice o' him that tells them quavers
    Just wi' fair fright.

And ye might tell, ayont the faem,
Thae Hieland clashes o' oor hame.
To speak the truth, I tak' na shame
    To half believe them;
And, stamped wi' TUSITALA's name,
    They'll a' receive them.

And folk to come, ayont the sea,
May hear the yowl of the Banshie,
And frae the water-kelpie flee,
    Ere a' things cease,
And island bairns may stolen be
    By the Folk o' Peace.

Faith, they might steal *me*, wi' ma will,
And, ken'd I ony Fairy hill,
I'd lay me down there, snod and still,
    Their land to win,
For, man, I've maistly had my fill
    O' this world's din.

The Fairy Minister.

IN MEMORY OF

The Rev. ROBERT KIRK,

WHO *WENT TO HIS OWN HERD*, AND ENTERED INTO
THE LAND OF THE PEOPLE OF PEACE,
IN THE YEAR OF GRACE SIXTEEN
HUNDRED AND NINETY-TWO,
AND OF HIS AGE
FIFTY-TWO.

———

People of Peace ! A peaceful man,
  Well worthy of your love was he,
Who, while the roaring Garry ran
  Red with the life-blood of Dundee,
While coats were turning, crowns were falling.
  Wandered along his valley still,
And heard your mystic voices calling
  From fairy knowe and haunted hill.
He heard, he saw, he knew too well
  The secrets of your fairy clan ;
You stole him from the haunted dell,
  Who never more was seen of man.
Now far from heaven, and safe from hell,
  Unknown of earth, he wanders free.
Would that he might return and tell
  Of his mysterious company !
For we have tired the Folk of Peace ;
  No more they tax our corn and oil ;
Their dances on the moorland cease,
  The Brownie stints his wonted toil.
No more shall any shepherd meet
  The ladies of the fairy clan,
Nor are their deathly kisses sweet
  On lips of any earthly man.
And half I envy him who now,
  Clothed in her Court's enchanted green,
By moonlit loch or mountain's brow
  Is Chaplain to the Fairy Queen.

A. L.

KIRK'S
SECRET COMMONWEALTH.

INTRODUCTION.

I. The History of the Book and Author.

The bibliography of the following little tract is extremely obscure. The title-page of the edition of 1815, which we reproduce, gives the date as 1691. Sir Walter Scott says in his *Demonology and Witchcraft* (1830, p. 163, note), "It was printed with the author's name in 1691, and reprinted, in 1815, for Longman & Co." But was there really a printed edition of 1691? Scott says that he never met with an example. Research in our great libraries has discovered none, and there is none save that of 1815 at Abbotsford. The reprint, of one hundred copies, was made, as it states, from no printed text, but from "a manuscript copy preserved in the Advocates' Library." On page 45 of the edition of 1815,

at the end of the comments on Lord Tarbott's
Letters, there is a " Note by the Transcriber "
—that is, the person who wrote out the manuscript in the Advocates' Library : " See the rest
in a little manuscript belonging to Coline Kirk."
Now Coline or Colin Kirk, Writer to the Signet,
was the son of the Rev. Mr. Kirk, author of the
tract. If the son had his father's book only in
manuscript, it seems very probable that it was
not printed in 1691 ; that the title-page is only
the title-page of a manuscript. Till some printed
text of 1691 is discovered, we may doubt, then,
whether the hundred copies published in 1815,
and now somewhat rare, be not the original
printed edition. The editor has a copy of 1815,
but it is the only one which he has met with
for sale.

The Rev. Robert Kirk, the author of *The
Secret Commonwealth*, was a student of theology
at St. Andrews : his Master's degree, however,
he took at Edinburgh. He was (and this is
notable) the youngest and *seventh* son of Mr.
James Kirk, minister of Aberfoyle, the place
familiar to all readers of *Rob Roy*. As a seventh
son, he was, no doubt, specially gifted, and in
The Secret Commonwealth he lays some stress on

the mystic privileges of such birth.   There may be "some secret virtue in the womb of the parent, which increaseth until the seventh son be borne, and decreaseth by the same degree afterwards."   It would not surprise us if Mr. Kirk, no less than the Rev. Robert Blair of St. Andrews (1650–60), could heal scrofula by the touch, like royal persons—Charles III. in Italy, for example.   As is well known to all, the House of Brunswick has no such powers. However this may have been, Mr. Kirk was probably drawn, by his seventh sonship, to a more careful study of psychical phenomena than most of his brethren bestowed.   Little is known of his life.   He was minister originally of Balquidder, whence, in 1685, he was transferred to Aberfoyle.   This was no Covenanting district, and there is no bigotry in Mr. Kirk's dissertation.   He was employed on an "Irish" translation of the Bible, and he published a Psalter in Gaelic (1684).   He married, first, Isobel, daughter of Sir Colin Campbell of Mochester, who died in 1680, and, secondly, the daughter of Campbell of Fordy: this lady survived him. From his connection with Campbells, we may misdoubt him for a Whig.   By his first wife he had a son, Colin Kirk, W.S.; by his second wife, a son who was minister of Dornoch. He died (if he did die, which is disputed) in 1692, aged about fifty-one; his tomb was inscribed—

ROBERTUS KIRK, A.M.

Linguæ Hiberniæ Lumen.

The tomb, in Scott's time, was to be seen in the east end of the churchyard of Aberfoyle; but the ashes of Mr. Kirk *are not there*. His successor, the Rev. Dr. Grahame, in his *Sketches of Picturesque Scenery*, informs us that, as Mr. Kirk was walking on a *dun-shi*, or fairy-hill, in his neighbourhood, he sunk down in a swoon, which was taken for death. "After the ceremony of a seeming funeral," writes Scott (*op. cit.*, p. 105), "the form of the Rev. Robert Kirk appeared to a relation, and commanded him to go to Grahame of Duchray. 'Say to Duchray, who is my cousin as well as your own, that I am not dead, but a captive in Fairyland; and only one chance remains for my liberation. When the posthumous child, of which my wife has been delivered since my disappearance, shall be brought to baptism, I will appear in the room, when, if Duchray shall throw over my head the knife or dirk which he holds in his hand, I may be restored to society; but if this is neglected, I am lost for ever.'" True to his tryst, Mr. Kirk did appear at the christening, and "was visibly seen;" but Duchray was so astonished that he did not throw his dirk over the head of the appearance, and to society Mr. Kirk has not yet been restored. This is extremely to be regretted, as he could now add matter of much importance to his treatise. Neither history nor tradition has more to tell about Mr. Robert Kirk, who seems to have been a man of good family, a student, and, as his book shows, an innocent and learned person.

II. The Secret Commonwealth.

The tract, of which the reader now knows the history, is a little volume of somewhat singular character. Written in 1691 by the Rev. Robert Kirk, minister of Aberfoyle, it is a kind of metaphysic of the Fairy world. Having lived through the period of the sufferings of the Kirk, the author might have been expected either to neglect Fairyland altogether, or to regard it as a mere appanage of Satan's kingdom—a "burning question" indeed, for some of the witches who suffered at Presbyterian hands were merely narrators of popular tales about the state of the dead. That she trafficked with the dead, and from a ghost won a medical recipe for the cure of Archbishop Adamson of St. Andrews, was the charge against Alison Pearson. "The Bischope keipit his castle lyk a tod in his holl, seik of a disease of grait fetiditie, and oftymes under the cure of women suspected of witch-craft, namlie, ane wha confessit hir to haiff learnit medecin of ane callit Mr. Wilyeam Sim-sone, that apeired divers tymes to hir efter his dead, and gaiff hir a buik. . . . She was execut in Edinbruche for a witch" (James Melville's *Diary,* p. 137, 1583). The Archbishop, like other witches, had a familiar in the form of a hare, which once ran before him down the street. These were the beliefs of men of learn-ing like James, the nephew and companion of Andrew Melville. Even in our author's own time, Archbishop Sharp was accused of enter-taining "the muckle black Deil" in his study at midnight, and of being "levitated" and dancing in the air. This last feat, creditable to a saint or a Neo-Platonist like Plotinus, was reckoned for

sin to Archbishop Sharp, as may be read in
Wodrow's *Analecta*. Thus all Fairydom was
commonly looked on as under the same guilt as
witchcraft. Yet Mr. Kirk of Aberfoyle, living
among Celtic people, treats the land of faery as
a mere fact in nature, a world with its own
laws, which he investigates without fear of the
Accuser of the Brethren. We may thus regard
him, even more than Wodrow, as an early
student in folk-lore and in psychical research
—topics which run into each other—and he
shows nothing of the usual persecuting disposition. Nor, again, is Mr. Kirk like Glanvil
and Henry More. He does not, save in his
title-page and in one brief passage, make super-
stitious creeds or psychical phenomena into
arguments and proofs against modern Sadducees.
Firm in his belief, he treats his matter in a
scientific spirit, as if he were dealing with
generally recognised physical phenomena.

Our study of Mr. Kirk's little tractate must
have a double aspect. It must be an essay
partly on folk-lore, on popular beliefs, their relation to similar beliefs in other parts of the
world, and the residuum of fact, preserved by
tradition, which they may contain. On the

other hand, as mental phenomena are in question—such things as premonitions, hallucinations, abnormal or unusual experiences generally—a criticism of Mr. Kirk must verge on "Psychical Research." The Society organised for that difficult subject certainly takes a vast deal of trouble about all manner of odd reports and strange visions. It "transfers" thoughts of no value, at a great expense of time and of serious hard work. But, as far as the writer has read the Society's Proceedings, it "takes no keep," as Malory says, of these affairs in their historical aspect. Whatever hallucination, or illusion, or imposture, or the "subliminal self" can do to-day, has always been done among peoples in every degree of civilisation. An historical study of the topic, as contained in trials for witchcraft, in the reports of travellers and missionaries, in the works of the seventeenth-century Platonists, More, Glanvill, Sinclair, and others, and in the rare tracts such as *The Devil in Glen Luce* and *The Just Devil of Woodstock*, not to mention Lavater, Wierus, Thyræus, Reginald Scott, and so on, is as necessary to the psychologist as to the folk-lorist.[1] If there be an element of fact

[1] Note (*a*), p. 81.

in modern hypnotic experiments (a matter on which I have really no opinion), it is plain that old magic and witchcraft are not mere illusions, or not commonplace illusions. The subliminal self has his stroke in these affairs. Assuredly the Psychologists should have an historical department. The evidence which they would find is, of course, vitiated in many obvious ways, but the evidence contains much that coincides with that of modern times, and the coincidence can hardly be designed—that is to say, the old Highland seers had no design of abetting modern inquiry. It may be, however, that their methods and ideas have been traditionally handed down to modern "sensitives" and "mediums." At all events, here is an historical chapter, if it be but a chapter in "The History of Human Error." These wide and multifarious topics can only be touched on lightly in this essay ; the author will be content if he directs the attention of students with more leisure and a better library of *diablerie* to the matter. But first we glance at *The Secret Commonwealth* as folk-lorists.

III. "THE SUBTERRANEAN INHABITANTS."

Mr. Kirk's first chapter, " Of the Subterranean Inhabitants," naturally suggests the recent speculations of Mr. MacRitchie. The gist of Mr. MacRitchie's *Testimony of Tradition* is that there once was a race of earth-dwellers in this island ; that their artificial caves still exist ; that this people survive in popular memory as "the legendary Feens," and as the Pechts of popular tales, in which they are regarded as dwarfs. "The Pechs were unco wee bodies, but terrible strang." Here, then, it might be thought that we have the origin of Fairy beliefs. There really was, on this showing, a dwarf race, who actually did live in the "fairy-hills," or howes, now commonly looked on as sepulchral monuments.

There is much in Mr. MacRitchie's theory which does not commend itself to me. The modern legends of Pechts as builders of Glasgow Cathedral, for example, do not appear to prove such a late survival of a race known as Picts, but are on a level with the old Greek belief that the Cyclopes built Mycenæ (*Testimony of Tradition*, p. 72). Granting, for the sake of discussion,

that there were still Picts or Pechs in Galloway
when Glasgow Cathedral was built (in the
twelfth century), these wild Galloway men,
scourges of the English Border, were the very
last people to be employed as masons. The
truth is that the recent Scotch have entirely
forgotten the ages of mediæval art. Accustomed
to the ill-built barns of a robbed and stinted
Kirk, they looked on the Cathedral as no work
of ordinary human beings. It was a creation
of the Pechts, as Mycenæ and Tiryns of the
mighty walls were creations of the Cyclopes.
By another coincidence, the well-known story
of the last Pecht, who refuses to divulge the
secret of the heather ale, is told in the Volsunga
Saga, and in the *Nibelungenlied*, of the Last
Niflung. Again, the breaking of a bar of iron,
which he takes for a human arm, by the last
Pecht is a tale current of the Drakos in modern
Greece (see Chambers's *Popular Traditions of
Scotland* for the last Pecht). I cannot believe
that the historical Picts were a set of half-
naked, dwarfish savages, hairy men living underground. These are the topics of Sir Arthur
Wardour and Monkbarns. Mr. W. F. Skene
may be said to have put the historic Picts in

their proper place as the ancestors of the Highlanders. The Pecht of legend answers to the
Drakos and the Cyclopes : the beliefs about his
habits may have been suggested by the tumuli,
still more by the *brochs:* it seems less probable
that they represent an historical memory. As
to the Irish "Feens," the topic can only be discussed by Celtic scholars. But it does not follow,
because the leader of the Feens seemed a dwarf
among giants, that therefore his people were a
dwarfish race.[1] The story proves no more than
Gulliver's Travels.

Once more, we often read in the Sagas of a
hero like Grettir, who opens a howe, has a
conflict with a "barrow-wight," as Mr. Morris
calls the "howe-dweller," and wins gold and
weapons. But the dweller in the howe is often
merely the able-bodied ghost of the Norseman,
a known and named character, who is buried
there ; he is not a Pecht. Thus, as it seems to
me, the Scotch and Celts possessed a theory of
a legendary people, as did the Greeks. Whether
any actual traditions of an earlier, perhaps a
Finnish race, was at the bottom of the legend,
is an obscure question. But, having such a

[1] *The Testimony of Tradition,* p. 75.

belief, the Scotch easily discovered homes for
the fancied people in the sepulchral howes:
they "combined their information." The Fairies,
again, are composite creatures. As they came
to births and christenings, and as Norse wise-
wives (as in the Saga of Eric the Red) prophesied at festivals, Mr. MacRitchie combines his
own information. The Wise-wife is a Finn
woman, and Finn and Fairy amalgamate. But
the Egyptians, as in the *Tale of Two Brothers*
(Maspero, *Contes Egyptiens*), had their Hathors,
who came and prophesied at births; the Greeks
had their Mœræ, as in the story of Meleager
and the burning brand. The Hathors and
Mœræ play, in ancient Egypt and in ancient
Greece, the part of Fairies at the christening,
but surely they were not Finnish women! In
short, though a memory of some old race may
have mingled in the composite Fairy belief, this
is at most but an element in the whole, and the
part played by ancestral spirits, naturally earth-
dwellers, is probably more important. Bishop
Callaway has pointed out, in the preface to his
Zulu Tales, that what the Highlanders say of
the Fairies the Zulus say of "the Ancestors."
In many ways, as when persons carried off to

Fairyland meet relations or friends lately deceased, who warn them, as Persephone and Steenie Steenson were warned, to eat no food in this place, Fairyland is clearly a memory of the pre-Christian Hades. There are other elements in the complex mass of Fairy tradition, but Chaucer knew "the Fairy Queen Proserpina," as Campion calls her, and it is plain that in very fact "the dread Persephone," the "Queen over death and the dead," had dwindled into the lady who borrows Tamlane in the ballad. Indeed Kirk mentions but does not approve of this explanation, "that those subterranean people are departed souls." Now, as was said, the dead are dwellers under earth. The worshippers of Chthonian Demeter (Achaia) beat the earth with wands; so does the Zulu sorcerer when he appeals to the Ancestors. And a Macdonald in Moidart, being pressed for his rent, beat the earth, and cried aloud to his dead chief, "Simon, hear me; you were always good to me."[1]

[1] In Father Macdonald's book on Moidart.

IV. FAIRYLAND AND HADES.

Thus, to my mind at least, the *Subterranean Inhabitants* of Mr. Kirk's book are not so much a traditional recollection of a real dwarfish race living underground (a hypothesis of Sir Walter Scott's), as a lingering memory of the Chthonian beings, "the Ancestors." A good case in point is that of Bessie Dunlop, of Dalry, in Ayrshire, tried on 8th November 1576 for witchcraft. She dealt in medicine and white magic, and obtained her prescriptions from Thomas Reid, slain at Pinkie fight (1547), who often appeared to her, and tried to lead her off to Fairyland. She, like Alison Pearson, was "convict and burnt" (Scott's *Demonology*, p. 146, and Pitcairn's *Criminal Trials*). Both ladies knew the Fairy Queen, and Alison Pearson beheld Maitland of Lethington, and Buccleugh, in Fairyland, as is recounted in a rhymed satire on Archbishop Adamson (Dalzell's *Scottish Poems*, p. 321). These are excellent proofs that Fairyland was a kind of Hades, or home of the dead.

Mr. Kirk, who speaks of the *Sleagh Maith* as confidently as if he were discussing the habits of some remote race which he has visited, credits

them, as the Greek gods were credited, with
the power of nourishing themselves on some fine
essential part of human sacrifice, of human food,
"some fine spirituous Liquors, that peirce like
pure Air and Oil, on the poyson or substance of
Corns and Liquors." Others, more gross, steal
the actual grain, "as do Crowes and Mice."
They are heard hammering in the howes: as
Brownies they enter houses and cleanse the
hearths. They are the Domovoys, as the Rus-
sians call them. John Major, in his exposition
of St. Matthew (1518, fol. xlviii.), gives perhaps
the oldest account of Brownies, in a believing
temper. Major styles them Fauni or *brobne.*
They thrash as much grain in one night as
twenty men could do. They throw stones about
among people sitting by the fire. Whether they
can predict future events is doubtful (see Mr.
Constable in Major's *Greater Britain,* p. xxx.
Edinburgh, 1892). To us they seem not much
remote from the Roman Lares—spirits of the
household, of the hearth. In all these creatures
Mr. Kirk recognises "an abstruse People," who
were before our more substantial race, whose
furrows are still to be seen on the hill-tops.
They never were, to his mind, plain palpable

folk; they are only visible, in their quarterly flittings, to men of the second sight. That gift of vision includes not only power to see distant or future events, but the viewless forms of air. To shun the flittings, men visit church on the first Sunday of the quarter: then they will be hallowed against elf-shots, "these Arrows that fly in the dark." As is well known, superstition explained the Neolithic arrow-heads as Fairy weapons; it does not follow that a tradition of a Neolithic people suggested the belief in Fairies. But we cannot deny absolutely that some such memory of an earlier race, a shy and fugitive people who used weapons of stone, may conceivably play its part in the Fairy legend.

Thence Mr. Kirk glides into that singular theory of savage metaphysics which somewhat resembles the Platonic doctrine of Ideas. All things, in Red Indian belief, have somewhere their ideal counterpart or "Father." Thus a donkey, when first seen, was regarded as "the Father" or archetype "of Rabbits." Now the second-sighted behold the "Double-man," "Doppel-ganger," "Astral Body," "Wraith," or what you will, of a living person, and that is merely his counterpart in the abstruse world. The

industry of the Psychical Society has collected
much material—evidence, whatever its value, for
the existence of the Double-man. We may call it
a hallucination, which does not greatly increase
our knowledge. From personal experience, and
the experience of friends, I am constrained to
believe that we may think we see a person who
is not really present to the view—who may be
in the next room, or downstairs, or a hundred
miles off. This experience has occurred to the
sane, the unimaginative, the healthy, the free
from superstition, and in circumstances by no
means mystic—for example, when the person
supposed to be seen was not dying, nor distressed,
nor in any but the most normal condition. Indeed, the cases when there was nothing abnormal
in the state of the person seen are far more
numerous, in my personal knowledge, than those
in which the person seen was dying, or dead, or
excited. The reverse appears to be the rule in
the experience of the Psychical Society. "The
actual proportion of coincidental to non-coinci-
dental cases, after all deduction for possible
sources of error, was in fact such that the pro-
bability against the supposition of chance coincidence became enormous, on the assumption of

ordinary accuracy on the part of informants"
(Professor Sidgwick, *Proc. S.P.R.*, vol. viii.
p. 607). Some 17,000 answers were collected.
We must apparently accept these facts as not
very abnormal nor very unusual, and doubtless as capable of some subjective explanation. But when such things occurred among
imaginative and uneducated Highlanders, they
became foundations and proofs of the doctrine
of second sight—proofs, too, of the primitive
metaphysical doctrine of counterparts and *corre-
spondances*. "They avouch that every Element
and different state of Being have Animals resem-
bling these of another Element." By persons
not knowing this, "the Roman invention of
guardian Angels particularly assigned" has been
promulgated. The guardian Angel of the Roman
superstition is merely the Double or Co-walker
—the type (in the viewless world) of the man
in the apparent world. Thus are wraiths and
ghosts explained by our Presbyterian psychologist and his Highland flock. All things univer-
sally have their types, their reflex : a man's
type, or reflex, or "co-walker" may be seen at a
distance from or near him during his life—nay,
may be seen after his death. The gifted man of

second sight can tell the substantial figure from
the airy counterpart. Sometimes the reflex
anticipates the action of the reality : "was often
seen of old to enter a House, by which the people
knew that the Person of that Likeness was to
visit them in a few days." It may have occurred
to most of us to meet a person in the street
whom we took for an acquaintance. It is not
he, but we meet the real man a few paces farther
on. Thus a distinguished officer, at home on
leave, met a friend, as he tells me, in Piccadilly.
The other passed without notice : the officer
hesitated about following him, did not, and in
some fifty yards met his man. There is probably no more in this than resemblance and
coincidence, but this is the kind of thing which
was worked by the Highlanders into their metaphysics.[1]

The end of the Co-walker is obscure. "This

[1] A much odder case is reported. Two young men
photographed a reach of a river. In the photograph,
when printed, was visible the dead body of a woman
floating on the stream. The water was dragged. Nothing
was found ; but two or three days later a girl drowned
herself in the pool ! As the Reports of the Psychical
Society sometimes say, "no confirmation has been obtained ; " but this is a pleasing instance of the Reflex,
and of second sight in a photographic camera.

Copy, Echo, or living Picture goes att last to his own Herd." Thus Ghosts are short-lived, and, according to M. d'Assier on the Manners of Posthumous Man (*L'Homme Posthume*), seldom survive for more than a century. By an airy being of this kind the Highlanders explained the false or morbid appetite. A "joint-eater" inhabited the patient; "he feeds two when he eats." As a rule, the Fairies get their food as witches do—take "the Pith and Milk from their Neighbours' Cows unto their own chiesehold, throw a Hair-tedder, at a great distance, by Airt Magic, only drawing a spigot fastened in a Post, which will bring Milk as farr as a Bull will be heard to roar." This is illustrated in the drinking scene in *Faust*. This kind of charge is familiar in trials for witchcraft.

In accordance with the whole metaphysics of the system of doubles, which are parasites on humanity, is the superstition of nurses stolen by Fairies, and of children kidnapped while changelings are left in their place. The latter accounts for sudden decline and loss of health by a child; he is not the original child, but a Fairy brat. To guard against this, bread (as human food hateful to Fairies—so the Kanekas carry a boiled

yam about at night), or the Bible, or iron is
placed in the bed of childbirth. "Iron scares
spirits," as the scholiast says of the drawn sword
of Odysseus in Hades. The Fairy bride, in
Wales, vanishes on being touched with iron.
This belief probably came in when iron was a
new, rare, and mysterious metal. The mortal
nurses in Fairyland are pleasantly illustrated by
the ballad

> "I heard a cow lowe,
>   A bonny, bonny cow lowe,"

in C. Kirkpatrick Sharpe's *Ballad Book*.[1] This
part of the superstition is not easy to elucidate.
Kirk repeats the well-known tales of the blinding
of the mortal who saw too clearly "by making
use of their Oyntments." Well-known examples
occur in Gervase of Tilbury, and are cited in
Scott's note on *Tamlane* in the *Border Min-
strelsy*. As Homer fables of the dead, their
speech is a kind of whistling like the cry of
bats—another indication of the pre-Christian
Hades.[2] They have feasts and burials; and
Pashley, in his *Travels in Crete*, tells the well-
known Border story of a man who fired on a

---

[1] It is also published in Mrs. Graham Tomson's *Border
Ballads* (Walter Scott).
[2] Note (*b*), p. 81.

Fairy bridal, and heard a voice cry, "Ye have slain the bonny bridegroom." It is, of course, to be noted that the modern Greek superstition of the Nereids, who carry off mortal girls to dance with them till they pine away, answers to some of our Fairy legends, while it will hardly be maintained that the Nereids are a memory of pre-historic Finns. "Antic corybantic jollity" is a note of Nereids, as well as of the *Sleagh Maith.* "The Inconvenience of their *succubi,*" the Fairy girls who make love to young men, is well known in the Breton ballad, *Le Sieur Nan.* The same superstition is current among the Kanekas of New Caledonia. My cousin, Mr. Atkinson, was visited by a young Kaneka, who twice or thrice returned to take leave of him with much emotion. When Mr. Atkinson asked what was the matter, the lad said that he had just met, as he thought, the girl of his heart in the forest. After a scene of dalliance she vanished, and he knew that she was a forest Fairy, and that he must die in three days, which he did. This is the "inconvenience of their succubi," regretted by Mr. Kirk. Thus it appears that the mass of these opinions is not local, nor Celtic merely, but of world-wide diffusion. Thus Sir Walter Scott observes of the Afghans and Highlanders, "Their superstitions are the same, or nearly so. The *Gholée Beabacan* (demons of the desert) resemble the *Boddach* of the Highlanders, 'who walked the heath at midnight and at noon'" (*Quarterly Review*, xiv. 289). Again, Mr. Kirk says that "Were-wolves and Witches' true Bodies are (by the union of the spirit of Nature that runs thorow all, echoing and doubling the Blow towards another) wounded at home, when the astrial or assumed Bodies are stricken elsewhere." Thus, if a witch-hare is shot, the witch's real body is hurt in the same part; and Lafitau, in North America, found that when a Huron shot a witch-bird, the real magician was stricken in the same place. The theory that the Fairies appear as "a little rough Dog" is illustrated by the Welsh Dogs of Hell. *Blackwood's Magazine* for 1818 contains many examples of these Hell-dogs, which are often invested in a sheet of fire, as Rink says is the case among the Eskimo. Take a modern instance. "Mr. F. A. Paley and friend, walking home at night on a lonely road, see a large black dog rise from it, slowly walk to the side, and disappear. They search in vain. Mr. Paley hears subsequently that this mysterious dog is the terror of the neighbourhood, but no such real dog is known." Date, summer 1837 (*Journ. of S.P.R.*, Feb. 1893, p. 31).

The dwellings of these airy shadows of mankind are, naturally, "Fairie Hills." There is such a hill, the Fairy Hill at Aberfoyle, where Mr. Kirk resided : Baillie Nicol Jarvie describes its legends in an admirable passage in *Rob Roy*. Mr. MacRitchie says, "How much of this 'howe' is artificial, or whether any of it is, remains to be discovered." It is much larger than most artificial tumuli. According to Mr. Kirk, the Highlanders "superstitiously believe the souls of their Predecessors to dwell" in the fairy-hills. "And for that end, say they, a Mote or Mount was dedicate beside every Churchyard, to receive the souls till their adjacent bodies arise, and so become as a Fairy hill." Here the Highland philosophers have conspicuously put the cart before the horse. The tumuli are much older than the churches, which were no doubt built beside them because the place had a sacred character. Two very good examples may be seen at Dalry, on the Ken, in Galloway, and at Parton, on Loch Ken. The grassy howes are

large and symmetrical, and the modern Presbyterian churches occupy old sites; at Parton
there are ruins of the ancient Catholic church.
Round the tumulus at Dalry, according to the
local form of the *Märchen* of Hesione, a great
dragon used to coil in triple folds, before it was
killed by the blacksmith. Nobody, perhaps,
can regard these tumuli, and many like them,
as anything but sepulchral. On the road between
Balantrae, in Ayrshire, and Stranraer, there is a
beautiful tumulus above the sea, which at once
recalls the barrow above the main that Elpenor
in the *Odyssey*, asked Odysseus to build for him,
"the memorial of a luckless man." In the
Argonautica of Apollonius Rhodius, the ghost
of a hero who fell at Troy appears to the adven-
turers on a tumulus like this of the Ayrshire
coast. In speaking of these barrows Mr. Kirk
tells how, during a famine about 1676, two
women had a vision of a treasure hid in a fairy-
hill. This they excavated, and discovered some
coins " of good money." The great gold corslet
of the British Museum is said to have been
found in Wales, where tradition spoke of a ghost
in golden armour which haunted a hillock. The
hillock was excavated, and the golden corslet,

like the Shakespearian bricks, is "alive to testify" to the truth of the story.

V. Fairies and Psychical Research.

The Fairy belief, we have said, is a composite thing. On the materials given by tradition, such as the memory, perhaps, of a pre-historic race, and by old religion, as in the thoughts about the pre-Christian Hades, poetry and fancy have been at work. Consumption, lingering disease, unexplained disappearances, sudden deaths, have been accounted for by the agency of the Fairies, or People of Peace. If the superstition included no more than this, we might regard it as a natural result of imagination, dealing with facts quite natural in the ordinary course of things. But there are elements in the belief which cannot be so easily dismissed. We must ask whether the abnormal phenomena which have been so frequently discussed, fought over, forgotten, and revived, do not enter into the general mass of folk-lore. They appear most notably in the two branches of Browniedom—of "Pixies," as they say in Devonshire, who haunt the house, and in the

alleged examples of the second sight. The
former topic is the more obscure, if not the
more curious. Let us examine the occurrences,
then, which may have begotten the belief in
Brownies, and in house-haunting Pixies or
Fairies. These appearances may be alleged, on
one hand, to be actual facts in Nature, the
workings of some yet unexplained forces; or
they may merely be the consequences of some
very old traditional method of imposture, vulgar
in itself, but still historical. That form of imposture, again, may be wrought either by conscious agents, or unconsciously and automatically
by persons under the influence of somnambulism ;
or, finally, the phenomena may in various cases
be due to any one of these three agencies, all of
which may possibly be *veræ causæ*, as conscious
imposture and trickery is certainly one *vera
causa.*

In Mr. Kirk's book we meet "the invisible
Wights which haunt Houses, . . . throw great
Stones, Pieces of Earth and Wood at the Inhabitants," but "hurt them not at all." As we
have said, Major (1518) calls these wights
"Fauni or Brobne"—that is, Brownies—and
says that they thrash as much grain in one

night as twenty men could do, and throw stones about. The legend of their working was common in Scotland, and a correspondent says that in Devonshire the belief in Pixies who set the house in order exists among the grand-parents of the present generation. But the sportive is more common than the kindly aspect of Brownies. Through history we constantly find them causing objects to move without visible contact, and "acting in sport, like Buffoons and Drolls." In his *Letters on Demonology* (p. 377) Scott gives instances where the buffoon or droll was detected, and confessed that the rattlings of plates and movements of objects were caused by an apparatus of threads or horse-hair. He also quotes the famous doings of "The Just Devil of Woodstock" in 1649, which so perplexed and discomfited the Cromwellian Commissioners. He accounts for those annoyances by the confessions of Joe Collins of Oxford, "Funny Joe," which he quotes from Hone's *Every-Day Book*, while Hone quotes from the *British Magazine* of 1747. But the writer in the *British Magazine* gives no references or authorities for the authenticity of Funny Joe's confessions, nor even for the existence of Joseph.

Scott could not find his original in the pamphlets
of the British Museum, and some of the state-
ments attributed to Joe do not tally with the
official account, and other contemporary docu-
ments collected in Sir Walter's *Woodstock*. Joe
pretends, for example, to have been secretary to
the Commission under the name of Giles Sharpe ;
but in the other accounts the secretary is named
Browne. A Royalist Brownie or Polter-geist
lies under shrewd suspicion, but Joe's own
existence is unproved, and his alleged evidence
is of no value. However, no sane person can
dream of doubting that many a Brownie has
been as much in flesh and blood as the Brownie
of Bodsbeck in Hogg's story.

There remain the less easily explicable tales
of strange and humorous disturbances, accompanied by loud sounds, rappings, the moving of
objects without visible contact, and so forth.[1]
Perhaps we may best examine these by taking
modern instances, collected by the Psychical
Society, in the first place, and then comparing
them with cases recorded at distant times and
in remote places. Some curious common features

---

[1] Many instances may be read of in a little anonymous
work, *Obeah*. The scene is Hayti.

will be observed, and the evidence has at least
the value of undesigned coincidence. Glanvil,
Telfair (minister of Rerrick), the Wesleys, Dr.
Adam Clarke, Increase Mather, were not modern
students of psychical research. The modern
Psychical Researchers, we fear, are not students
of old legendary lore, which they dismiss on
evidence not first-hand nor scientifically valid.
Thus they do not seem to be aware that they
are describing, almost in identical terms, phenomena identical with those noted by Telfair,
Mather, Lavater, and the rest, and by those
ancients attributed to devils. The modern re-
corders are not consciously copying from old
accounts ; the coincidences therefore have their
value, as proving that certain phenomena have
occurred and recurred. Now those phenomena
may be due to conscious or to hysterical imposture, but they have been frequent and common
enough to keep alive, and probably to originate,
a part of the Fairy belief—that part which is
concerned with Brownies and house-haunting
Pixies, or Domovoys. These, again, correspond
to the tricky beings described by Mr. Leland in
his *Etruscan Remains* as survivals of old Roman
and Etruscan popular religions, while we find

similar occurrences in the Empire of the Incas
not long after the Spanish conquest of Peru.[1]

Beginning, then, with what is nearest to us in
time, we take Mr. F. W. H. Myers's essays " On
the Alleged Movement of Objects without Contact, occurring not in the Presence of a Paid
Medium."[2] The alleged phenomena are, of
course, as common as blackberries in the presence of paid mediums, but are to the last degree
untrustworthy. Even when there is no paid
medium present, the mere contagious excitement
which is said to be developed at *séances* makes
all that is thought to occur there a story to be
taken with plenty of salt.[3] One of Mr. Myers's
examples was the result of *séances*, but it had
features of great importance for the argument.
It will be found in *Proc. S. P. R.*, vol. xix. p. 189,
July 1891. The performers are Mr. C., Mrs.
C., and Mr. H. Mr. C. and Mrs. C. are spoken
of as good witnesses, known to Mr. Myers and
Professor Barrett. Mr. H.'s health has suffered
so much that he cannot be examined, and Mr.

[1] Note (c), p. 82.
[2] *Proc. S. P. R.*, July 1891, February 1892.
[3] As far as the author has watched *séances* personally,
they have ended in nothing but "giggling and making
giggle."

H. is the person who interests us here, for reasons which will be given later. All three were "unbelievers" in these matters. On the second evening "lights floated about the room," which was lit, apparently, by a full moon. "F." (who is also "H.") felt cold hands touching, and "hands" recur in the old pre-scientific accounts. The three mages were holding hands tightly at the time. Now Mr. H. had hitherto been in excellent health, but after his chair was dragged from under him, and he was "thrown down on the ground," he went into "a trance." His watch and ring (on the finger of a hand held by Mrs. C.) were carried to a remote part of the room. H. leaves the circle and sits at the window. Another figure walks through the room. H. returns, is "thrown down," his coat is dragged off, and his boots are discovered on a distant sofa. He asks for "something from home," goes into a trance, a photograph locked up by him at home is found on the table. His wife, in town, "being quite ignorant of our having had *séances*, told us that, at that very hour, a fearful crash occurred in his bedroom. The photograph vanished, and returned last night, when H. was in a trance." He is "thrown

down" again.   He has "alternate fits of uncon-
sciousness and raving delirium."   The home of
Mr. and Mrs. C. (not the house where they sat)
is vexed by "figures," noises, knockings; "we
were sprinkled with water in the night," haunted
by sounds of drums and horns, and so forth.
Before a "manifestation," "we all felt a sudden
chill, like either a wave of intensely cold air
passing, or a rapid decrease of temperature." [1]

This is a disgusting story if Mr. H.'s health
was ruined by his presence at the performances.
The point, however, is that he did behave in
epileptic fashion while these events were in
progress.   It is natural to suppose that, in his
"trances," he may have been capable, unconsciously, of feats physically and morally impos-
sible to him in his normal condition.   This
explanation would not cover all the alleged occurrences, but would account for many of them.

---

[1] Some *séances* were held at —— College, Oxford,
about 1875. The performers were all athletic under-
graduates.   The breath of chill air was always felt
"before anything happened," and, when the out-college
men had gone, the owner of the rooms, in his bed-
chamber, was disturbed by the racket which continued
in the sitting-room.   But I know not if he had sported
his oak !

We now take an ancient instance, similar disturbances at Newberry, in New England, in 1679, similarly accompanied by the presence of an epileptic patient.[1] The house of William Morse was "strangely disquieted by a dæmon." The inmates were Morse, his wife, and their grandson, a boy whose age is not given. The trouble began on December 3, with a sound of heavy objects falling on the roof. On December 8, large stones and bricks "were thrown in at the west end of the house . . . the bedstead was lifted up from the floor, and the bed-staff flung out of the window, and a cat was hurled at the wife. A long staff danced up and down in the chimney. The man's wife put the staff in the fire, but she could not hold it there, inasmuch as it would forcibly fly out; yet after much ado, with joynt strength, they made it to burn. . . . A chair flew about, and at last lighted on the table, where victuals stood ready to eat, and was likely to spoil all, only by a nimble catching they saved some of their meat. . . . A chest was removed from place to place,

---

[1] *An Essay for the Recording of Illustrious Providences*, by Increase Mather. Boston, 1684; London, Reeves & Turner, 1890, pp. 101–111.

no hand touching it. Two keys would fly
about, making a loud noise by knocking against
each other. . . . As they lay in bed with their
little boy between them, a great stone from the
floor of the loft was thrown upon the man's
stomach, and he turning it down upon the floor,
it was once more thrown upon him." On January 23, 1680, "his ink-horn was taken away
from him while he was writing" (he was keeping
a diary of these events), "and when by all his
seeking he could not find it, at last he saw it
drop out of the air, down by the fire. . . .
February 2, while he and his boy were eating of
cheese, the pieces which he cut were wrested from
them. . . . But as for the boy, he was a great
sufferer in these afflictions, for on the 18th of
December he, sitting by his grandfather, was
hurried into great motions. The man made him
stand between his legs, but the chair danced
up and down, and was like to have cast both
man and boy into the fire, and the child was
tossed about in such a manner as that they
feared his brains would have been beaten out."

All these contortions of the boy were apparently what M. Charcot calls *clownisms.*[1] When

[1] *Diseases of the Nervous System,* iii. 249. London, 1890.

taken to a doctor's house the boy "was free of disturbances," which returned with his return home. He barked like a dog, clucked like a hen, talked nonsense about "Powel," who pinched and bullied him. While he was in bed with the old people, "a pot with its contents was thrown upon them." They were clutched by hands, like Mr. and Mrs. C. Once a voice was heard singing, "Revenge, revenge is sweet." Finally a mate of a ship came, declared that the grandmother was not rightly suspected as a witch, and offered, if he were left alone with the boy, to cure him. "The mate came next day betimes, and the boy was with him till night; since which time his house, Morse saith, has not been molested with evil spirits." Probably the mate used a rope's end: the boy was more speedily cured than Mr. H.

The phenomena are those of droll or buffooning wights, as Mr. Kirk says, and no man can doubt that the boy was at the bottom of the whole affair. But whether he was capable, when well and conscious, of such diversions, is another question. Children like him produced the famous witch-mania in New England.

We have here, undeniably, a well-recorded

case, analogous to that of Mr. H.   In a modern
case of bell-ringing, heavy thumps, and movement of objects, the agent was "a young girl
who had never been out to service before,"
and who passed the night in a state of wildly
agitated somnambulism, repeating the whole of
the Service for the day.[1]   Mather gives several
other examples, in which motives for trickery
are manifest, while we hear nothing of an epileptic or hysterical patient.

In the majority of instances, ancient or modern,
children are the agents.   Thus we have "Physical Phenomena obtained in a Family Circle,"
that of Mr. and Mrs. Davis, with their children,
at Rio Janeiro.[2]   The time was 1888.   Curiosity
had been caused by "the notorious Henry Slade."
There were "touches and grasps of hands."   A
table "ran after me" (Professor Alexander) "and
attempted to hem me in," when only C., a little
girl, was in the room.   "As far as I could see,
she did not even touch the table."   The chair
of Amy (aged thirteen months) was moved about,
like that of Master Morse two hundred years
earlier.   A table jumped into the laps of the

---

[1] *Proc. S. P. R.*, xix. 160–173.
[2] *Op. cit.*, pp. 173–189.

public. There were raps and thumps, which
"seemed to shake the whole building." Lights
floated about. A slate, covered with flour, was
placed on C.'s lap; her hands lay on the table.
Marks of fingers came on the flour, and, in
answer to request, the mark of "a naked baby
foot." The children present were wearing laced
boots, and we are not told that little Amy was
under the table. Bluish lights and the phantasm
of a dog were seen.

All this answers to an ancient example—the
disturbances in Mr. Wesley's house at Epworth,
December 1715 to January 1716.[1] The house
was a new one, rebuilt in 1709. We have Mr.
Samuel Wesley's Journal, with many contemporary letters from members of the family, and
later reminiscences. There were many lively
girls in the house, and two servants—a maid
and a man, recently engaged. The disturbances
began with groanings; then came knockings,
which flitted about the house. Mr. Wesley
heard nothing till December 21. The knocks
replied to those made by the family, but they
never could imitate the sounds. Mrs. Wesley

[1] *Memoirs of the Wesley Family*, by Adam Clarke,
LL.D., F.A.S. London, 1823, pp. 161–200.

and Emily saw an object "like a badger" run
from under a bed and vanish. The mastiff was
much alarmed by the sounds. Mr. Wesley was
"thrice pushed by invisible power." The bogie
was a Jacobite, as was Mrs. Wesley : Mr. Wesley
was for King George. The knocks were violent
when that usurper was prayed for. They did
not try praying for King James. Robin, the servant, saw a hand-mill work violently. "Naught
vexed me but that it was empty. I thought,
had it but been full of malt, he might have
ground his heart out for me." But this was a
jocose, not an industrious devil. Robin called
it "old Jeffries," after a gentleman lately dead ;
the family called it "Jeffrey," unless one name
is a mere misspelling. It "seemed to sweep
after" Nancy Wesley, when she swept the
chambers. "She thought he might have done
it for her, and saved her the trouble." Mrs.
Wesley concealed the matter from her husband,
"lest he should fancy it was against his own
death" (Letter of January 12, 1716–17). This
belief in noises foretelling death is very common ;
compare Scott's nocturnal disturbances at Abbotsford when Bullock, his agent in building it, was
dying in London. The racket occurred on April

28 and 29, 1818, and Scott examined the scene "with Beardie's broadsword under my arm."[1] Bullock died in Tenterden Street, in London, whether on April 28 or 29 is not easily to be ascertained. "The noise resembled half a dozen men putting up boards and furniture, and nothing can be more certain than that there was nobody on the premises at the time."[2] The noises used to follow Hetty Wesley, and thump under her feet, as under those of C. in Professor Alexander's narrative. Mr. Wesley's plate "danced before him on the table a pretty while, without anybody's stirring the table."[3] The disturbances quieted down in January, but recurred on March 31. Similar phenomena had occurred "long before" in the family.[4] "The sound very often seemed in the air, in the middle of a room, nor could they ever make any such themselves by any contrivance."[5] On February 16, 1740, twenty-three years later, Emily writes to Jack about "that *wonderful thing* called by us *Jeffrey*.

---

[1] Letter to Terry, April 30. Lockhart, v. 309.
[2] Scott to Terry, May 16.
[3] Susannah Wesley to Samuel Wesley, March 27, 1717.
[4] *Op. cit.*, p. 193.
[5] *Op. cit.*, p. 194.

. . . That something calls on me against any extraordinary new affliction."

Priestley styles this affair " the best-authenticated that is anywhere extant." He supposes it to have been "a trick of the servants, for mere amusement." The *modus operandi* is difficult to explain. We hear nothing of bad health or hysterics in the household.[1] For our purpose it is enough that a few incidents of this kind, however produced, might originate and keep alive the belief in Brownies, and

> "That shrewd and knavish sprite
> Called Robin Goodfellow,"

who

> "Frights the maidens of the villagery,
> Skims milk, and sometimes labours in the quern."

By a curious coincidence, we can show a case in which phenomena of the kind usually reported as occurring at *séances*, and in examples like that of William Morse, were actually accepted as manifestations of the *Sleagh Maith*, or Fairies. In his account of the disturbances in the Wesley family, Dr. Clarke, the author, averred that he had himself witnessed similar events. It thus became necessary to consult his *Life* (London,

---

[1] Note (*d*), p. 83.

1833). "In the history of my own life," says
Dr. Clarke, "I have related this matter in suffi-
cient detail."[1] Unluckily, in his *Life* (pp. 76,
77) he gives scarce any details. Previous to
sudden deaths in a family called Church, the
phenomena of falling plates, heavy tread, and
other noises occurred. Mr. Clarke "sat up one
whole night in the kitchen, and most distinctly
heard the above noises." He was a born mystic,
and even in childhood a reader of Cornelius
Agrippa, and, later, of the alchemists. But he
records the instance of a woman, who solemnly
declared to Mrs. Clarke that a number of the
gentle people (*Sleagh Maith*) "occasionally fre-
quented her house; that they often conversed
with her, one of them putting its hands on her
eyes during the time, which hands she repre-
sented, from the sensation she had, to be about
the size of those of a child of four or five years
of age." The family were "worn down" with
these visits, and from the mention of touches of
hands it is pretty plain that we have to do with
the kind of sprite who paws people at *séances*.
But these sprites are recognised (the scene is the
North of Ireland) as "gentle people," Folk of

[1] *Memoirs of the Wesley Family*, p. 198.

Peace. The amusing thing is, that Mr. Clarke, while he believes in Mr. Wesley's Jeffrey, and in the supernatural origin of a noise in a kitchen, laughs at similar phenomena when assigned to Fairies. It is a mere difference of terminology.

Another old example may be given. It is Alexander Telfair's "True Relation" of disturbances at Ringcroft, in the parish of Rerrick.[1] The story is attested by the signatures of Ewart, minister of Kells, in Galloway ; Monteith, minister of Borg ; Murdoch, minister of Crosmichael, on Loch Ken ; Spalding, minister at Parton, also by Loch Ken ; Falconer, minister at Keltown ; Mr. M'Lellan of Colline, Lennox of Milhouse, and a number of farmers. These were all neighbours, and all attested what they saw and heard. Robert Chambers says, "There never, perhaps, was any mystic history better attested. Few narrations of the kind have included occurrences and appearances which it was more difficult to reconcile with the theory of trick or imposture." Mr. Telfair himself had been

---

[1] Edinburgh : Mossman, 1696. There is a London reprint, of which I have a copy. The pamphlet is republished in Mr. Stevenson's edition of Sinclair's *Satan's Invisible World Discovered*, 1685-1871, Appendix, p. xix.

chaplain, in 1687, to Sir Thomas Kirkpatrick of Closeburn. He was then an Episcopalian.

Andrew Mackie was a stone-mason at Rerrick. On March 7 (1695?), and for long after, stones began to fly about in his house by night and day. "The stones which hit any person had not half their natural weight." Mackie complained to Telfair, his minister, who entered the house and prayed: nothing odd occurred. As he stood outside, he "saw two little stones drop down on the croft;" then he was asked to return, and was pelted inside the cottage. This was March 11. For a week there was no more trouble, then the disturbances began again. Mr. Telfair was sent for, and was pelted, beaten with a staff, and heard loud knockings. "That night, as I was at prayer, leaning on a bedside, I felt something lifting up my arm. I, casting my eyes thither, perceived a little white hand and arm from the elbow down, but presently it evanished." "There was never anything seen except that hand I saw," and an apparition of a boy in grey clothes. Sometimes the stoning went on in the open air.[1] There were plenty

---

[1] Compare similar phenomena in *Obeah*, and in Peruvian example, note (c), p. 82.

of touchings, grippings, and scratchings. "The door-bar" (a long, heavy piece of squared wood) "would go thorow the house as if a person were carrying it in their hand, yet nothing seen doing it." Here we compare, in *Proc. S. P. R.*, February 1892, the story of a carpenter's shop at Swanland, in Yorkshire, where pieces of wood were "levitated" into abnormal flight. No imposture was discovered, nor was the presence of any one person necessary.

The ministers of Kells and Crosmichael were pelted with stones of eight pounds weight. On April 6, fire-balls floated through the cottage. When five ministers were present, "it made all the house shake, brake a hole through the thatch, and poured in great stones." "It handled the legs of some as with a man's hand;" it hoisted Mr. Telfair, Lennox of Millhouse, and others off the ground! A sieve flew through the house; Mackie caught it; a force gripped it, and pulled the interior part out of the rim. A day of humiliation was solemnly kept in the parish, which only excited the emulation of the disturbing agent; "it continued in a most fearful manner without intermission." Voices were heard, which talked nonsense of a semi-scriptural kind; finally the thing died out early in May. By the way, on April 28, "it pulled down the end of the house, all the stone-work thereof."

This is a very odd case, as no suspicion is thrown on the children. The attestations of several witnesses are given, not only at the close, but for almost every separate incident. The vision of the white hand is agreeable.

The Devil of Glen Luce, in Galloway, was published by Sinclair in his *Hydrostaticks*, of all places, in 1672, and again in *Satan's Invisible World*, and by Glanvil in *Sadducismus Triumphatus*. In this affair a boy called Thomas, a son of the unlucky householder, was clearly the agent. The phenomena were stone-throwing, beating with sticks, levitation of a plate, and a great deal of voices, probably uttered by the aforesaid Thomas. The Synod ordered a day of humiliation (1655–56).

The affair of the Drummer of Tedworth (1661) is, or ought to be, too well known for quotation. The troubles began after Mr. Mompesson seized the drum of a vagrant musician. In the presence of a clergyman, chairs walked about the room of themselves, "a bed-staff was thrown at the minister, but so favourably that a lock of

wool could not have fallen more softly." The
children, as usual, were especially haunted. A
jingling of money was common, as it also was at
Epworth. Lights wandered about the house,
"blue and glimmering." The noise was persis-
tent in the woodwork of the children's beds,
while their hands were outside. The knocks
answered knocks made by visitors. There were
divers other marvels. The Drummer was suspected, but, consciously or not, the children
were probably the agents. They seem to have
been in their usual health.[1] In Galashiels (date
not given), loud knocks on the floor accompanied
a hystero-epileptic girl wherever she sat. In
bed, "her body was so lifted up that many
strong men were not able to keep it down."
The minister, who could make nothing of her,
was Mr. Wilkie; the girl was Margaret Wilson
(Sinclair, p. 200).

This little parcel of strange stories may suffice
to show that part of the Fairy belief is based on
such incidents as still occur, or are reported to
occur, just in the old fashion. It is for psychologists and physicians to ascertain how far, if at

---

[1] Glanvil's version is given in Sinclair's *Satan's Invisible World.*

all, the incidents are produced by hysterical, or
epileptic, or somnambulistic patients. Common
forthright trickery is usually detected in paid
mediums. But the trickery simulates real
events, or continues an old traditional form of
imposture. The moral that parents should not
allow their children to be present at *séances*
hardly needs enforcing. Some of them may
escape unharmed, but frightful injuries may be
inflicted on health and on character.[1]

VI. SECOND SIGHT AND "TELEPATHY."

We have already hinted that events of an
ordinary kind—illusions, cases of mistaken iden-
tity, or hallucination—are probably the ground-
work in part of the Highland belief in second
sight. Of course, if a certain proportion of
hallucinations were or could be taken for "veridical," attention would be given to these alone :
the others would be neglected. The Psychical
Society has collected and examined hundreds of
these cases in modern life.

The Society may find out, experimentally,
whether second sight can be acquired in the
manner described by Mr. Kirk—whether by

[1] Note (*e*), p. 85.

the hair tether, or by merely putting the foot
under that of a seer. Thus contact is used
in thought reading, as, in second sight, the
seer by contact communicates his hallucination.
Second sight itself is now called telepathy,
which, however, does not essentially advance
our knowledge of the subject. It is either very
common, or people who choose to claim the
possession of it are very common. In our
society it is mere matter for idle tales; in
the Highlands the second sight was a belief
and a system. Mr. Pepys and Dr. Johnson
investigated the matter, and Dr. Johnson came
away open to conviction, but unconvinced. The
Psychical Society is now examining second
sight in the Highlands. It is interesting to
learn that the Presbyterian seers justified their
visions out of the Bible, which also justified
the burning of these gifted men on occasion.
Mr. Kirk is tolerant enough to ascribe their
visions to a "bounty of Providence." This
may have passed, north of the Highland
line, but in Fife and the south the seers would
speedily have been accommodated with a stake
and tar-barrel. The writings of Wodrow and
Mr. Robert Blair of St. Andrews (1650–60)

prove that if a savoury preacher wrought marvels, he was inspired, but if an amateur did
the very same things, — prophesied, healed
diseases, and so forth,—he, or she, was likely
to be haled before the Presbytery, and possibly
dragged to the stake. In the Highlands these
invidious distinctions were less forcibly drawn.
Mr. Kirk treats the whole question in his
curiously cold scientific way. If these things
occur, they are in the realm of Nature, and are
results of causes which may be variously conjectured. They may be providential, or a sport
of evolution, derived from " a complexionall
Quality of the first acquirer," which often
becomes hereditary in his lineage.

Lord Tarbott's letter to an inquirer, Robert
Boyle, is added by Mr. Kirk to his little
treatise, with his own annotations. His belief
that the Fairy sights could only be seen while
the eyes are kept steady without twinkling, is
attested by a well-known anecdote. On the
afternoon of Culloden, a little girl, staying
with Lord Lovat at Gortuleg, was reading in
a window-seat. Chancing to look out, she saw
a company of headlong riders hastening to the
castle. Believing them to be the *Sleagh Maith*,

she tried hard to keep her eyes from twinkling, that she might not lose the vision. But these, alas! were no Fairies, they were Prince Charles and his men flying from the victorious English. The tale proves that the belief long survived the day of the minister of Aberfoyle. Lord Tarbott mentions, also, the vision of the shroud on the breast of a man about to die, which seems to be alluded to in the prophecy of Theoclymenus in the *Odyssey.* Lord Tarbott's tales are of the familiar kind, there are dozens of such in *Theophilus Insulanus.* Mr. Kirk's notes are chiefly remarkable for his citation of Walter Grahame's "evil eye," which killed what he praised,—a world-wide superstition, too common to need supporting by foreign and classical examples.

Unluckily, at this point Mr. Kirk abandons what we may call his scientific attitude. He has accounted for his "supernatural" affairs as not supernatural at all, but phenomena in Nature, and subject, like other phenomena, to laws. But now it occurs to him to explain the conduct of his *Sleagh Maith* as the result of missionary zeal on their part: "they endeavour to convince us of a Deity;" though, on the face

of his argument, a Co-walker no more proves a
Deity than does an ordinary "walker." He may
have been reading "the learned Dr. Mor" (More
the Platonist), and may have altered his ideas.
His account of a girl who learned, or rather
composed, a long poem by aid of "our nimble
and courteous spirits," affords an early example
of what is called "an inspirational medium."
It is unlucky that Mr. Kirk did not publish
this work, of which he had a copy. The ordinary "spiritual" poetry may be written, as Dr.
Johnson said of *Ossian*, "by any one who would
abandon his mind to it." When Mr. Kirk
maintains that Neolithic arrow-heads could not
have been executed "by all the Airt of man,"
he relapses from his usual odd common-sense.
He also believes in men who are magically shot-
proof, like Claverhouse, who had to be shot by a
silver bullet; like Archbishop Sharp, on whom
his pious assassins erroneously held that their
bullets took no effect; and like certain soldiers
mentioned by Dugald Dalgetty of Drumthwacket.
This absurd belief was very generally held by
the Covenanters. Where his local superstitions
and those of his generation are not concerned,
Mr. Kirk recovers his clearness of intellect. In

Purgatory he finds only the pre-Christian Hades,
"our Secret Republick," with an ecclesiastical
colouring—"additional Fictions of Monks' doting
and crazied Heads." Mr. Kirk did not perceive
the danger involved in his own argument. If
a Highland second-sighted man answers to a
Hebrew prophet in his visions and trances, a
Hebrew prophet is in danger of being no more
considered than a Highland second-sighted man.
However, it is to Mr. Kirk's praise that he shows
no persecuting disposition as far as witches are
concerned (though he has seen them pricked),
and that he argues very fairly from his premisses,
and within his limits.[1] He recognises the unity
of spiritual phenomena and of popular beliefs,
whether it springs from a common well-head of
delusion in our nature, or whether it really has
a source in the observation of peculiar and rather
rare phenomena.

To the Edinburgh edition of 1815 (probably
the only one) the editor added the work of
Theophilus Insulanus on Second Sight. This is
not rare nor expensive, and we do not reproduce
it. One case of "telepathy" may be quoted
from Theophilus.

[1] Note (*f*), p. 86.

"Donald Beaton, residenter in Hammir, related that, in his passage from Glasgow to the
Isle of Sky, he stopped at Tippermory, a known
harbour in the Isle of Mull." Here some one
gave him a loin of venison. Donald, whose
wife's mother was a seer, to try her powers,
wished that piece of venison in her hands.
"The same night the seer, who lived with her
daughter, his wife, apprehended she saw him
enter the house with a shapeless lump in his
hands—she knew not what, but it resembled
flesh, which gave herself and her daughter great
joy, as they had despaired of him by his long
absence." This is "telepathy," if telepathy
there be.

Another picturesque tale shows how, on the
night before the Rout of Moy, Patrick M'Caskill
met the famed M'Rimmon (*sic*), M'Leod's piper,
in the town of Inverness, and saw him contract
into the size of a boy of five or six, and expand
again into his athletic proportions. M'Rimmon
was killed in the Rout of Moy—an attempt to
surprise and seize Prince Charles. Before leaving
Skye he had prophesied—

"M'Leod shall come back,
But M'Rimmon shall never."

The editor is acquainted with a splendid case of second sight in Kensington. The seer was an accomplished English gentleman, and mentioned his vision at the moment to a witness who remembers and corroborates the statement. Thus the Hebrides and Highlands have no monopoly of second sight.

The researches of M. Charcot, M. Richet, and other psychologists do not at present help us much in the matter of veridical second sight. It is not a hallucination " suggested " to a hypnotised subject, but an impression produced by a remote person or event on a subject who has not been hypnotised at all. For example, Dr. Adam Clarke, in his *Life* (vol. ii. p. 16) tells us of Mr. Tracy Clarke, who, being in the Isle of Man with his son, dreamed that he had visited his wife in Liverpool. He told his son that Mrs. Clarke was looking very well, but, contrary to her habit, was sleeping in the best bedroom. On the day when Mr. Clarke said this, Mrs. Clarke, who had been sleeping in her best bedroom, told the little son who lay in her room that she had heard his father ride up to the house, stable his horse, open the door, come upstairs, and walk round her bed, but that she could not see him. This is a case at least of second hearing, and has no hypnotic explanation.

We end in the candid spirit of Dr. Johnson, as far as the Polter-Geist and second sight are concerned—willing to be convinced, but far indeed from conviction. As to the Fairy belief, we conceive it to be a complex matter, from which tradition, with its memory of earth-dwellers, is not wholly absent, while more is due to a survival of the pre-Christian Hades, and to the belief in local spirits—the Vuis of Melanesia, the Nereids of ancient and modern Greece, the Lares of Rome, the fateful Mœræ and Hathors—old imaginings of a world not yet "dispeopled of its dreams." [1]

[1] The "earth-houses" in Scotland and the isles, which seem to have been inhabited at an early period, can seldom be called hills or mounds ; being built for purposes of concealment, they are usually almost on a level with the surrounding land. The *Fairy hills*, on the other hand, are higher and much more notable, and were probably sepulchral. This, at least, is the impression left on me by Mr. MacRitchie's book, *The Underground Life.* (Privately printed. Edinburgh, 1892.)

Puss-in-Boots smells a rat.

AN ESSAY

OF

The Nature and Actions of the Subterranean (and,
for the moſt Part,) Inviſible People, heretofioir
going under the name of ELVES, FAUNES,
and FAIRIES, or the lyke, among the Low-
Country Scots, as they are deſcribed by thoſe
who have the SECOND SIGHT ; and now, to
occaſion further Inquiry, collected and com-
pared, by a Circumſpect Inquirer reſiding
among the Scottiſh-Iriſh in Scotland.

A

𝔖𝔢𝔠𝔯𝔢𝔱 𝔠𝔬𝔪𝔪𝔬𝔫𝔴𝔢𝔞𝔩𝔱𝔥,

OR,

A Treatife difplayeing the Chiefe Curiofities
as they are in Ufe among diverfe of the
People of Scotland to this Day;
SINGULARITIES for the
moft Part peculiar to
that Nation.

A Subject not heretofore difcourfed of by any of our
Writters; and yet ventured on in an Effay
to fupprefs the impudent and growing
Atheifme of this Age, and to
fatiffie the defire of fome
choice Freinds.

---

*Then a Spirit paffed before my Face, the Hair of my
Flefh ftood up; it ftood ftill, but I could not difcerne
the Forme thereof; ane Image was before mine Eyes.*
—Job, 4. 15, 16.

This is a REBELLIOUS PEOPLE, *which fay to the Siers, fie
not; and to the Prophets, prophefie not unto us right
Things, bot fpeak unto us fmoothe Things.*—Ifaiah,
30. 9, 10.

And the Man whofe Eyes were open hath faid.—Numbers, 24. 15.

*For now we fie thorough a Glafs darkly, but then Face to
Face.*—1 Corinth. 13. 12.

*It doth not yet appear what we fhall be; but we fhall be
lyke God, and fie him as he is.*—1 John, 3. 2.

Μη γιγαντες μαιωδησονται υποκατωδεν υδατος και των
γειτονων αυτον;—Job, 26. 5 (Septuag.).

By MR ROBERT KIRK, Minifter at Aberfoill.

1691.

CHAPTER I.

OF THE SUBTERRANEAN INHABITANTS.

THESE *Siths*, or FAIRIES, they call *Sleagh Maith*, or the Good People, it would feem, to prevent the Dint of their ill Attempts, (for the Irifh ufe to blefs all they fear Harme of;) and are faid to be of a midle Nature betuixt Man and Angel, as were Dæmons thought to be of old; of intelligent ftudious Spirits, and light changable Bodies, (lyke thofe called Aftral,) fomewhat of the Nature of a condenfed Cloud, and beft feen in Twilight. Thes Bodies be fo plyable thorough the Subtilty of the Spirits that agitate them, that they can make them appear or difappear att Pleafure. Some have Bodies or Vehicles fo fpungious, thin, and defecat, that they are fed by only fucking into fome fine fpirituous Liquors, that peirce lyke

pure

pure Air and Oyl: others feid more grofs on
the Foyfon or fubftance of Corns and Liquors,
or Corne it felfe that grows on the Surface of
the Earth, which thefe Fairies fteall away, partly
invifible, partly preying on the Grain, as do
Crowes and Mice; wherefore in this fame Age,
they are fome times heard to bake Bread, ftrike
Hammers, and do fuch lyke Services within the
little Hillocks they moft haunt: fome whereof
of old, before the Gofpell difpelled Paganifm,
and in fome barbarous Places as yet, enter
Houfes after all are at reft, and fet the Kitchens
in order, cleanfing all the Veffels. Such Drags
goe under the name of Brownies. When we
have plenty, they have Scarcity at their Homes;
and on the contrarie (for they are empowred to
catch as much Prey everywhere as they pleafe,)
there Robberies notwithftanding oft tymes oc-
caffion great Rickes of Corne not to bleed fo
weill, (as they call it,) or prove fo copious by
verie farr as wes expected by the Owner.

THERE Bodies of congealled Air are fome
tymes caried aloft, other whiles grovell in different Schapes, and enter into any Cranie or Clift

of

of the Earth where Air enters, to their ordinary
Dwellings; the Earth being full of Cavities and
Cells, and there being no Place nor Creature
but is fuppofed to have other Animals (greater
or leffer) living in or upon it as Inhabitants;
and no fuch thing as a pure Wildernefs in the
whole Univerfe.

2. WE then (the more terreftriall kind have
now fo numeroufly planted all Countreys,) do
labour for that abftrufe People, as weill as for
ourfelves. Albeit, when feverall Countreys were
unhabitated by ws, thefe had their eafy Tillage
above Ground, as we now. The Print of thofe
Furrous do yet remaine to be feen on the Shoulders of very high Hills, which was done when
the champayn Ground was Wood and Forreft.

THEY remove to other Lodgings at the Beginning of each Quarter of the Year, fo traverfing
till Doomfday, being imputent and [impotent
of?] ftaying in one Place, and finding fome Eafe
by fo purning [Journeying] and changing Habi-
tations. Their chamælion-lyke Bodies fwim in
the Air near the Earth with Bag and Bagadge;
and at fuch revolution of Time, SEERS, or Men

of

of the SECOND SIGHT, (Fæmales being feldome
fo qualified) have very terrifying Encounters
with them, even on High Ways; who therefoir
ufwally fhune to travell abroad at thefe four
Seafons of the Year, and thereby have made it
a Cuftome to this Day among the Scottifh-Irifh
to keep Church duely evry firft Sunday of the
Quarter to fene or hallow themfelves, their
Corns and Cattell, from the Shots and Stealth
of thefe wandring Tribes; and many of thefe
fuperftitious People will not be feen in Church
againe till the nixt Quarter begin, as if no Duty
were to be learned or done by them, but all the
Ufe of Worfhip and Sermons were to fave them
from thefe Arrows that fly in the Dark.[1]

THEY are diftributed in Tribes and Orders,
and have Children, Nurfes, Mariages, Deaths,
and Burialls, in appearance, even as we, (unlefs
they fo do for a Mock-fhow, or to prognofticate
fome fuch Things among us.)

3. THEY are clearly feen by thefe Men of the
SECOND SIGHT to eat at Funeralls [and] Ban-
quets; hence many of the Scottifh-Irifh will not
teaft

[1] Note (*a*), p. 86.

teaſt Meat at theſe Meittings, leſt they have
Communion with, or be poyſoned by, them.
So are they ſeen to carrie the Beer or Coffin
with the Corps among the midle-earth Men to
the Grave. Some Men of that exalted Sight
(whither by Art or Nature) have told me they
have ſeen at theſe Meittings a Doubleman, or
the Shape of ſome Man in two places; that is,
a ſuperterranean and a ſubterranean Inhabitant,
perfectly reſembling one another in all Points,
whom he notwithſtanding could eaſily diſtinguiſh
one from another, by ſome ſecret Tockens and
Operations, and ſo go ſpeak to the Man his
Neighbour and Familiar, paſſing by the Apparition or Reſemblance of him. They avouch that
every Element and different State of Being have
Animals reſembling theſe of another Element;
as there be Fiſhes ſometimes at Sea reſembling
Monks of late Order in all their Hoods and
Dreſſes; ſo as the Roman invention of good and
bad Dæmons, and guardian Angells particularly
aſſigned, is called by them an ignorant Miſtake,
ſprung only from this Originall. They call this
Reflex-man a Co-walker, every way like the
Man,

Man, as a Twin-brother and Companion, haunt-
ing him as his fhadow, as is oft feen and known
among Men (refembling the Originall,) both
before and after the Originall is dead ; and wes
alfo often feen of old to enter a Hous, by which
the People knew that the Perfon of that Liknes
wes to Vifite them within a few days. This
Copy, Echo, or living Picture, goes att laft to his
own Herd. It accompanied that Perfon fo long
and frequently for Ends beft known to it felfe,
whither to guard him from the fecret Affaults of
fome of its own Folks, or only as ane fportfull
Ape to counterfeit all his Actions. However,
the Stories of old WITCHES prove beyond con-
tradiction, that all Sorts of People, Spirits which
affume light aery Bodies, or crazed Bodies co-
acted by forrein Spirits, feem to have fome
Pleafure, (at leaft to affwage from Pain or
Melancholy,) by frifking and capering like
Satyrs, or whiftling and fcreeching (like un-
lukie Birds) in their unhallowed Synagogues
and Sabboths. If invited and earneftly re-
quired, thefe Companions make themfelves
knowne and familiar to Men ; other wife, being
in

in a different State and Element, they nather
can nor will eafily converfe with them. They
avouch that a Heluo, or Great-eater, hath a
voracious Elve to be his attender, called a
Joint-eater or Juft-halver, feeding on the Pith
or Quinteffence of what the Man eats ; and that
therefoir he continues Lean like a Hawke or
Heron, notwith ftanding his devouring Appetite : yet it would feem that they convey that
fubftance elfewhere, for thefe Subterraneans eat
but little in their Dweliings ; there Food being
exactly clean, and ferved up by Pleafant Children, lyke inchanted Puppets. What Food they
extract from us is conveyed to their Homes by
fecret Paths, as fume fkilfull Women do the Pith
and Milk from their Neighbours Cows into their
own Chiefe-hold thorow a Hair-tedder, at a great
Diftance, by Airt Magic, or by drawing a fpickot
faftened to a Poft, which will bring milk as farr
of as a Bull will be heard to roar.[1] The Chiefe
made of the remaineing Milk of a Cow thus
ftrain'd will fwim in Water like a Cork. The
Method they take to recover their Milk is a
bitter

[1] Note (*b*), p. 87.

bitter chyding of the fufpetted Inchanters,
charging them by a counter Charme to give
them back their own, in God, or their Mafter's
Name.   But a little of the Mother's Dung
ftroakit on the Calves Mouth before it fuck
any, does prevent this theft.

4. THEIR Houfes are called large and fair,
and (unlefs att fome odd occafions) unperceave-
able by vulgar eyes, like Rachland, and other
inchanted Iflands, having fir Lights, continual
Lamps, and Fires, often feen without Fuel to
fuftain them.   Women are yet alive who tell
they were taken away when in Child-bed to
nurfe Fairie Children, a lingering voracious
Image of their (them?) being left in their place,
(like their Reflexion in a Mirrour,) which (as if
it were fome infatiable Spirit in ane affumed
Bodie) made firft femblance to devour the
Meats that it cunningly carried by, and then
left the Carcafe as if it expired and departed
thence by a naturall and common Death.   The
Child, and Fire, with Food and other Necef-
faries, are fet before the Nurfe how foon fhe
enters ; but fhe nather perceaves any Paffage
                                                    out

out, nor fees what thofe People doe in other Rooms of the Lodging. When the Child is wained, the Nurfe dies, or is conveyed back, or gets it to her choice to ftay there. But if any Superterraneans be fo fubtile, as to practice Slights for procuring a Privacy to any of their Mifteries, (fuch as making ufe of their Oyntments, which as Gygef's Ring makes them invifible, or nimble, or cafts them in a Trance, or alters their Shape, or makes Things appear at a vaft Diftance, &c.) they fmite them without Paine, as with a Puff of Wind, and bereave them of both the naturall and acquired Sights in the twinkling of ane Eye, (both thefe Sights, where once they come, being in the fame Organ and infeparable,) or they ftrick them Dumb. The Tramontains to this Day put Bread, the Bible, or a piece of Iron, in Womens Beds when travelling, to fave them from being thus ftollen; and they commonly report, that all uncouth, unknown Wights are terrifyed by nothing earthly fo much as by cold Iron. They delyver the Reafon to be that Hell lying betwixt the chill Tempefts, and the Fire Brands of fcalding

Metals

Metals, and Iron of the North, (hence the
Loadſtone cauſes a tendency to that Point,)
by ane Antipathy thereto, theſe odious far-
ſcenting Creatures ſhrug and fright at all that
comes thence relating to ſo abhorred a Place,
whence their Torment is eather begun, or
feared to come hereafter.

5. THEIR Apparell and Speech is like that
of the People and Countrey under which they
live : ſo are they ſeen to wear Plaids and varie-
gated Garments in the Highlands of Scotland,
and Suanochs therefore in Ireland. They ſpeak
but litle, and that by way of whiſtling, clear,
not rough. The verie Divels conjured in any
Countrey, do anſwer in the Language of the
Place ; yet ſometimes the Subterraneans ſpeak
more diſtinctly than at other times. Ther
Women are ſaid to Spine very fine, to Dy,
to Toſſue, and Embroyder : but whither it is
as manuall Operation of ſubſtantiall refined
Stuffs, with apt and ſolid Inſtruments, or only
curious Cob-webs, impalpable Rainbows, and
a fantaſtic Imitation of the Actions of more
terreſtricall Mortalls, ſince it tranſcended all
                                              the

the Senfes of the Seere to difcerne whither, I
leave to conjecture as I found it.

6. THERE Men travell much abroad, either
prefaging or aping the difmall and tragicall
Actions of fome amongft us; and have alfo many
difaftorous Doings of their own, as Convoca-
tions, Fighting, Gafhes, Wounds, and Burialls,
both in the Earth and Air. They live much
longer than wee; yet die at laft, or [at] leaft
vanifh from that State. 'Tis ane of their Tenets,
that nothing perifheth, but (as the Sun and
Year) every Thing goes in a Circle, leffer or
greater, and is renewed and refrefhed in its
Revolutions; as 'tis another, that every Bodie
in the Creation moves, (which is a fort of Life;)
and that nothing moves, but [h]as another
Animal moving on it; and fo on, to the utmoft
minuteft Corpufcle that's capable to be a Receptacle of Life.

7. THEY are faid to have ariftocraticall Rulers
and Laws, but no difcernible Religion, Love,
or Devotion towards God, the bleffed Maker
of all: they difappear whenever they hear his
Name invoked, or the Name of JESUS, (at
which

which all do bow willinglie, or by conſtraint,
that dwell above or beneath within the Earth,
Philip. 2. 10;) nor can they act ought at that
Time after hearing of that ſacred Name. The
TABHAISVER, or Seer, that correſponds with
this kind of Familiars, can bring them with a
Spel to appear to himſelfe or others when he
pleaſes, as readily as Endor Witch to thoſe of
her Kind. He tells, they are ever readieſt to
go on hurtfull Errands, but ſeldome will be the
Meſſengers of great Good to Men. He is not
terrified with their Sight when he calls them,
but ſeeing them in a ſurpryze (as often he does)
frights him extreamly. And glaid would he be
quite of ſuch, for the hideous Spectacles ſeen
among them ; as the torturing of ſome Wight,
earneſt ghoſtly ſtairing Looks, Skirmiſhes, and
the like. They do not all the Harme which
appearingly they have Power to do; nor are
they perceaved to be in great Pain, ſave that
they are uſewally ſilent and ſullen. They are
ſaid to have many pleaſant toyiſh Books; but
the operation of theſe Peices only appears in
ſome Paroxiſms of antic corybantic Jolity, as if
                                    raviſht

ravifht and prompted by a new Spirit entering into them at that Inftant, lighter and mirrier than their own. Other Books they have of involved abftrufe Senfe, much like the Rofurcian [Rofycrucian] Style. They have nothing of the Bible, fave collected Parcells for Charms and counter Charms; not to defend themfelves withall, but to operate on other Animals, for they are a People invulnerable by our Weapons; and albeit Were-wolves and Witches true Bodies are (by the union of the Spirit of Nature that runs thorow all, echoing and doubling the Blow towards another) wounded at Home, when the aftrial affumed Bodies are ftricken elfewhere; as the Strings of a Second Harp, tune to ane unifon, Sounds, though only ane be ftruck; yet thefe People have not a fecond, or fo grofs a Bodie at all, to be fo pierced; but as Air, which when divyded units againe; or if they feel Pain by a Blow, they are better Phyficians than wee, and quickly cure it. They are not fubject to fore Sickneffes, but dwindle and decay at a certain Period, all about ane Age. Some fay their continual Sadnefs is becaufe of

B   their

their pendulous State, (like thofe Men, Luc. 13.
2. 6.) as uncertain what at the laft Revolution
will become of them, when they are lock't up
into ane unchangeable Condition; and if they
have any frolic Fitts of Mirth, 'tis as the con-
ftrained grinning of a Mort-head, or rather as
acted on a Stage, and moved by another, ther
[than?] cordially comeing of themfelves. But
other Men of the Second Sight, being illiterate,
and unwary in their Obfervations, learn from
thofe; one averring thofe fubterranean People
to be departed Souls, attending awhile in this
inferior State, and clothed with Bodies procured
throwgh their Almfdeeds in this Lyfe; fluid,
active, ætheriall Vehicles to hold them, that
they may not fcatter, or wander, and be loft in
the Totum, or their firft Nothing; but if any
were fo impious as to have given no Alms, they
fay when the Souls of fuch do depairt, they
fleep in an unaictve State till they refume the
terreftriall Bodies again : others, that what the
Low-countrey Scotts calls a Wreath, and the
Irish Taibhshe[1] or Death's Meffenger, (appearing

1 The *Death-candle* is called Druig.

pearing fometimes as a little rough Dog, and if croffed and conjured in Time, will be pacified by the Death of any other Creature inftead of the fick Man,) is only exuvious Fumes of the Man approaching Death, exhal'd and congeal'd into a various Liknefs,[1] (as Ships and Armies are fometimes fhapt in the Air,) and called aftral Bodies, agitated as Wild-fire with Wind, and are neather Souls or counterfeiting Spirits; yet not a few avouch (as is faid,) that furelie thefe are a numerous People by them felves, having their own Polities. Which Diverfities of Judgments may occafion feverall Inconfonancies in this Re-hearfall, after the narroweft Scrutiny made about it.

8. THEIR Weapons are moft what folid earthly Bodies, nothing of Iron, but much of Stone, like to yellow foft Flint Spa, fhaped like a barbed Arrow-head, but flung like a Dairt, with great Force. Thefe Armes (cut by Airt and Tools it feems beyond humane) have fomething of the Nature of Thunderbolt fubtilty, and mortally wounding the vital Parts without breaking the Skin; of which Wounds I have obferved in

Beafts,

[1] Note (*c*), p. 87.

Beafts, and felt them with my Hands. They are not as infallible Benjamites, hitting at a Hair's-breadth; nor are they wholly unvanquifh-able, at leaft in Appearance.

THE MEN of that SECOND SIGHT do not dif-cover ftrange Things when afked, but at Fits and Raptures, as if infpyred with fome Genius at that Inftant, which before did lurk in or about them. Thus I have frequently fpoke to one of them, who in his Tranfport told he cut the Bodie of one of thofe People in two with his Iron Weapon, and fo efcaped this Onfet, yet he faw nothing left behind of that appear-ing divyded; at other Times he out wrefted [wreftled?] fome of them. His Neibours often perceaved this Man to difappear at a certane Place, and about one Hour after to become vifible, and difcover him felfe near a Bow-fhot from the firft Place. It was in that Place where he became invifible, faid he, that the Subter-raneans did encounter and combate with him. Thofe who are unfeened or unfanctified (called Fey) are faid to be pierced or wounded with thofe People's Weapons, which makes them do
somewhat

fomewhat verie unlike their former Practice, caufing a sudden Alteration, yet the Caufe thereof unperceavable at prefent; nor have they Power (either they cannot make ufe of their natural Powers, or afk't not the heavenly Aid,) to efcape the Blow impendent. A Man of the Second Sight perceaved a Perfon standing by him (found to others view) wholly gored in Blood, and he (amazed-like) bid him inftantly flee. The whole Man laught at his Airt and Warning, fince there was no appearance of Danger. He had fcarce contracted his Lips from Laughter, when unexpectedly his Enemy leapt in at his Side, and ftab'd him with their Weapons. They alfo pierce Cows or other Animals, ufewally faid to be Elf-fhot, whofe pureft Subftance (if they die) thefe Subterraneans take to live on, viz. the aereal and ætherial Parts, the moft fpirituous Matter for prolonging of Life, fuch as Aquavitæ (moderately taken) is among Liquors, leaving the terreftrial behind. The Cure of fuch Hurts is, only for a Man to find out the Hole with his Finger; as if the Spirits flowing from a Man's

warme

warme Hand were Antidote fufficient againft
their poyfon'd Dairts.

9. As Birds and Beafts, whofe Bodies are
much ufed to the Change of the frie and open
Air, forfee Storms; fo thofe invifible People
are more fagacious to underftand by the Books
of Nature Things to come, than wee, who are
peftered with the groffer Dregs of all elementary
Mixtures, and have our purer Spirits choaked
by them. The Deer fcents out a Man and
Powder (tho a late Invention) at a great Diftance; a hungry Hunter, Bread; and the Raven,
a Carrion: Ther Brains, being long clarified by
the high and fubtil Air, will obferve a very fmall
Change in a Trice. Thus a Man of the Second
Sight, perceaving the Operations of thefe fore-
cafting invifible People among us, (indulged
thorow a ftupendious Providence to give Warnings of fome remarkable Events, either in the
Air, Earth, or Waters,) told he faw a Winding-
fhroud creeping on a walking healthful Perfons
Legs till it come to the Knee; and afterwards
it came up to the Midle, then to the Shoulders,
and at laft over the Head, which was vifible to

no

no other Perfone. And by obferving the Spaces of Time betwixt the feverall Stages, he eafily gueffed how long the Man was to live who wore the Shroud; for when it approached his Head, he told that fuch a Perfon was ripe for the Grave.

10. THERE be many Places called Fairie-hills, which the Mountain People think impious and dangerous to peel or difcover, by taking Earth or Wood from them; fuperftitioufly be-leiving the Souls of their Prediceffors to dwell there.[1] And for that End (fay they) a Mote or Mount was dedicate befide every Church-yard, to receive the Souls till their adjacent Bodies arife, and fo become as a Fairie-hill; they ufe-ing Bodies of Air when called Abroad. They alfo affirme thofe Creatures that move invifibly in a Houfe, and caft hug great Stones, but do no much Hurt, becaufe counter-wrought by fome more courteous and charitable Spirits that are everywhere ready to defend Men, (Dan. 10. 13.) to be Souls that have not attained their Reft, thorough a vehement Defire of revealling a Murther or notable Injurie done or receaved,

or

[1] Note (*d*), p. 88.

or a Treafure that was forgot in their Liftyme
on Earth, which when difclof'd to a Conjurer
alone, the Ghoft quite removes.

IN the nixt Country to that of my former
Refidence, about the Year 1676, when there
was fome Scarcity of Graine, a marvelous Illapfe
and Vifion ftrongly ftruck the Imagination of
two Women in one Night, living at a good
Diftance from one another, about a Treafure
hid in a Hill, called SITHBHRUAICH, or Fayrie-
hill. The Appearance of a Treafure was firft
reprefented to the Fancy, and then an audible
Voyce named the Place where it was to their
awaking Senfes. Whereupon both arofe, and
meitting accidentallie at the Place, difcovered
their Defigne; and joyntly digging, found a
Veffell as large as a Scottifh Peck, full of fmall
Pieces of good Money, of ancient Coyn; which
halving betuixt them, they fold in Difh-fulls for
Difh-fulls of Meall to the Countrey People.
Very many of undoubted Credit faw, and had
of the Coyn to this Day. But whither it was a
good or bad Angell, one of the fubterranean
People, or the reftlefs Soul of him who hid it,
                                                that

that difcovered it, and to what End it was done,
I leave to the Examination of others.

11. THESE Subterraneans have Controverfies,
Doubts, Difputs, Feuds, and Siding of Parties;
there being fome Ignorance in all Creatures,
and the vafteft created Intelligences not com-
paffing all Things. As to Vice and Sin, whatever their own Laws be, fure, according to ours,
and Equity, natural, civil, and reveal'd, they
tranfgrefs and commit Acts of Injuftice, and
Sin, by what is above faid, as to their ftealling
of Nurfes to their Children, and that other fort
of Plaginifm in catching our Children away,
(may feem to heir fome Eftate in thofe invifible
Dominions,) which never returne. For the
Inconvenience of their Succubi, who tryft with
Men, it is abominable; but for Swearing and
Intemperance, they are not obferved fo fubject
to thofe Irregularities, as to Envy, Spite, Hypo-
cracie, Lieing, and Diffimulation.

12. As our Religion oblidges us not to make
a peremptory and curious Search into thefe
Obftrufeneffes, fo that the Hiftories of all Ages
give as many plain Examples of extraordinary
Occurrances

Occurrances as make a modeſt Inquiry not con-
temptable.   How much is written of Pigme's,
Fairies, Nymphs, Syrens, Apparitions, which tho
not the tenth Part true, yet could not ſpring
of nothing !   Even Engliſh Authors relate (of)
Barry Iſland, in Glamorganſhire, that laying
your Ear into a Clift of the Rocks, blowing
of Bellows, ſtricking of Hammers, claſhing of
Armour, fyling of Iron, will be heard diſtinctly
ever ſince Merlin inchaunted thoſe ſubterranean
Wights to a ſolid manuall forging of Arm's to
Aurelius Ambroſius and his Brittans, till he
returned ; which Merlin being killed in a Battell,
and not coming to looſe the Knot, theſe active
Vulcans are there ty'd to a perpetuall Labour.
But to dip no deeper into this Well, I will nixt
give ſome Account how the Seer my Informer
comes to have this ſecret Way of Correſpondence
beyond other Mortalls.

THERE be odd Solemnities at inveſting a
Man with the Priviledges of the whole Miſtery
of this Second Sight.   He muſt run a Tedder
of Hair (which bound a Corps to the Bier) in a
Helix [?] about his Midle, from End to End ;
                                                                 then

then bow his Head downwards, as did Elijah,
1 Kings, 18. 42. and look back thorough his
Legs untill he fie a Funerall advance till the
People crofs two Marches; or look thus back
thorough a Hole where was a Knot of Fir.
But if the Wind change Points while the Hair
Tedder is ty'd about him, he is in Peril of his
Lyfe. The ufewall Method for a curious Perfon
to get a tranfient Sight of this otherwife invifible
Crew of Subterraneans, (if impotently and over
rafhly fought,) is to put his [left Foot under the
Wizard's right] Foot, and the Seer's Hand is
put on the Inquirer's Head, who is to look
over the Wizard's right Shoulder, (which hes
ane ill Appearance, as if by this Ceremony ane
implicit Surrender were made of all betwixt
the Wizard's Foot and his Hand, ere the Perfon
can be admitted a privado to the Airt;) then
will he fee a Multitude of Wight's, like furious
hardie Men, flocking to him haiftily from all
Quarters, as thick as Atoms in the Air; which
are no Nonentities or Phantafms, Creatures
proceiding from ane affrighted Apprehenfione,
confufed or crazed Senfe, but Realities, appearing

ing to a ſtable Man in his awaking Senſe, and
enduring a rationall Tryall of their Being.   Thes
thorow Fear ſtrick him breathleſs and ſpeechleſs.
The Wizard, defending the Lawfullneſs of his
Skill, forbids ſuch Horror, and comforts his
Novice by telling of Zacharias, as being ſtruck
ſpeechleſs at ſeeing Apparitions, Luke, 1. 20.
Then he further maintains his Airt, by vouching
Eliſha to have had the ſame, and difcloſ'd it
thus unto his Servant in 2 Kings, 6. 17. when
he blinded the Syrians ; and Peter in Act, 5. 9.
forſeing the Death of Saphira, by perceaving as
it were her Winding-ſheet about her before
hand ; and Paul, in 2nd Corinth. 12. 4. who
got ſuch a Viſion and Sight as ſhould not, nor
could be told.   Eliſha alſo in his Chamber ſaw
Gehazi his Servant, at a great Diſtance, taking
a reward from Naaman, 2d Kings, 5. 26.
Hence were the Prophets frequently called
SEERS, or Men of a 2d or more exhalted Sight
than others.   He acts for his Purpoſe alſo
Math. 4. 8. where the Devil undertakes to give
even Jeſus a Sight of all Nations, and the fineſt
Things in the World, at one Glance, tho in
their

their naturall Situations and Stations at a vaſt Diſtance from other. And 'tis ſaid expreſly he did let ſie them; not in a Map it ſeems, nor by a phantaſtick magicall jugling of the Sight, which he could not impoſe upon ſo diſcovering a Perſon. It would appear then to have been a Sight of real ſolid Subſtances, and Things of worth, which he intended as a Bait for his Purpoſe. Whence it might ſeem, (compairing this Relation of Math. 4. 8. with the former,) that the extraordinary or Second Sight can be given by the Miniſtery of bad as weill as good Spirits to thoſe that will embrace it. And the Inſtance of Balaam and the Pytheniſs make it nothing the leſs probable. Thus alſo the Seer trains his Scholler, by telling of the Grada-tions of Nature, ordered by a wiſe Provydence; that as the Sight of Bats and Owls tranſcend that of Shrews and Moles, ſo the viſive Faculties of Men are clearer than thoſe of Owls; as Eagles, Lynxs, and Cats are brighter than Mens. And again, that Men of the Second Sight (being deſigned to give warnings againſt ſecret Engyns) ſurpaſs the ordinary Viſion of other

Men

Men, which is a native Habit in fome, defcended
from their Anceftors, and acquired as ane artificiall Improvement of their natural Sight in
others; refembling in their own Kynd the
ufuall artificiall Helps of optic Glaffes, (as Pro-
fpectives, Telefcopes, and Microfcopes,) without
which afcititious Aids thofe Men here treated
of do perceive Things that, for their Smallnefs,
or Subtility, and Secrecy, are invifible to others,
tho dayly converfant with them; they having
fuch a Beam continuallie about them as that
of the Sun, which when it fhines clear only,
lets common Eyes fee the Atomes, in the Air,
that without thofe Rayes they could not difcern;
for fome have this Second Sight tranfmitted
from Father to Sone thorow the whole Family,
without their own Confent or others teaching,
proceeding only from a Bounty of Providence
it feems, or by Compact, or by a complexionall
Quality of the firft Acquirer. As it may feem
alike ftrange (yet nothing vicious) in fuch as
Mafter Great-rake,[1] the Irifh Stroaker, Seventh-
fons, and others that cure the King's Evill,

and

---

[1] Note (*e*), p. 88.

and chafe away Defeafes and Pains, with only ftroaking of the affected Pairt; which (if it be not the Reliques of miraculous Operations, or fome fecret Virtue in the Womb, of the Parent, which increafeth until Seventh-fons be borne, and decreafeth by the fame Degrees after-wards,) proceids only from the fanitive Bal-fome of their healthfull Conftitutions; Virtue going out from them by fpirituous Effluxes un-to the Patient, and their vigorous healthy Spirits affecting the fick as ufewally the unhealthy Fumes of the fick infect the found and whole.

13. THE Minor Sort of Seers prognofticat many future Events, only for a Month's Space, from the Shoulder-bone of a Sheep on which a Knife never came, (for as before is faid, and the Nazarits of old had fomething of it) Iron hinders all the Opperations of those that travell in the Intrigues of thefe hidden Dominions. By looking into the Bone, they will tell if Whoredom be committed in the Owner's Houfe; what Money the Mafter of the Sheep had; if any will die out of that Houfe for that Moneth; and if any Cattell there will take a Trake, as

if

if Planet-ftruck. Then will they prefcribe a Prefervative and Prevention.

14. A WOMAN (it feems ane Exception from the generall Rule,) fingularlie wife in thefe Matters of Foirfight, living in Colafnach, ane Ifle of the Hebrides, (in the Time of the Mar-quefs of Montrofe his Wars with the States in Scotland,) being notorious among many; and fo examined by fome that violently feazed that Ifle, if fhe faw them coming or not? She faid, fhe faw them coming many Hours before they came in View of the Ifle. But earneftly look-ing, fhe fome times took them for Enemyes, fometime for Friends; and morover they look't as if they went from the Ifle, not as Men ap-proaching it, which made her not put the In-habitants on their Guard. The Matter was, that the Barge wherein the Enemie failed, was a little befoir taken from the Inhabitants of that fame Ifle, and the Men had their Backs towards the Ifle, when they were plying the oares towards it. Thus this old Scout and Delphian Oracle was at leaft deceived, and did deceave. Being afked who gave her fuch Sights and

and Warnings, fhe faid, that as foon as fhe fet three Croffes of Straw upon the Palm of her Hand, a great ugly Beaft fprang out of the Earth neer her, and flew in the Air. If what fhe enquired had Succefs according to her Wifh, the Beaft would defcend calmly, and lick up the Croffes. If it would not fucceid, the Beaft would furioufly thruft her and the Croffes over on the Ground, and fo vanifh to his Place.

15. AMONG other Inftances of undoubted Verity, proving in thefe the Being of fuch aerial People, or Species of Creatures not vulgarly known, I add the fubfequent Relations, fome whereof I have from my Acquaintance with the Actors and Patients, and the Reft from the Eye-witneffes to the Matter of Fact. The firft whereof fhall be of the Woman taken out of her Child-bed, and having a lingring Image of her fubftituted Bodie in her Roome, which Refemblance decay'd, dy'd, and was bur'd. But the Perfon ftollen returning to her Hufband after two Years Space, he being convinced by many undenyable Tokens that fhe

c   was

was his former Wyfe, admitted her Home, and
had diverſe Children by her.   Among other
Reports ſhe gave her Huſband, this was one :
That ſhe perceived litle what they did in the
ſpacious Houſe ſhe lodg'd in, untill ſhe anointed
one of her Eyes with a certain Unction that
was by her ; which they perceaving to have
acqainted her with their Actions, they fain'd
her blind of that Eye with a Puff of their
Breath.   She found the Place full of Light,
without any Fountain or Lamp from whence
it did ſpring.   This Perſon lived in the Countrey nixt to that of my laſt Reſidence, and
might furniſh Matter of Diſpute amongſt Caſuiſts,
whither if her Huſband had been mary'd in the
Interim of her two Years Abſence, he was
oblidged to divorſe from the ſecond Spouſe at
the Return of the firſt.   There is ane Airt,
appearingly without Superſtition, for recovering
of ſuch as are ſtolen, but think it ſuperfluous
to inſert it.

I ſaw a Woman of fourtie Years of Age,
and examined her (having another Clergie Man
in my Companie) about a Report that paſt of
her

her long fafting [*her Name is not intyre.*][1] It was told by them of the Houfe, as well as her felfe, that fhe tooke verie little or no Food for feverall Years paft; that fhe tarried in the Fields over Night, faw and converfed with a People fhe knew not, having wandered in feeking of her Sheep, and fleep't upon a Hillock, and finding her felf tranfported to another Place before Day. The Woman had a Child fince that Time, and is ftill prettie melanchollyous and filent, hardly ever feen to laugh. Her natural Heat and radical Moifture feem to be equally balanced, lyke ane unextinguifhed Lamp, and going in a Circle, not unlike to the faint Lyfe of Bees, and fome Sort of Birds, that fleep all the Winter over, and revive in the Spring.

IT is ufuall in all magicall Airts to have the Candidates prepoffeffit with a Believe of their Tutor's Skill, and Ability to perform their Feats, and act their jugling Pranks and Legerdemain; but a Perfon called Stewart, poffeffed with a prejudice at that was fpoken of the 2d Sight,

[1] Thus in the Manuscript, which is only a Transcript of Mr. Kirk's Original. Perhaps M'Intyre?

and

and living near to my Houfe, was foe put to it
by a Seer, before many Witneffes, that he loft
his Speech and Power of his Legs, and breath-
ing exceffively, as if expyring, becaufe of the
many fearfull Wights that appeared to him.
The Companie, were forced to carrie him into
the Houfe.

IT is notorioufly known what in Killin, within
Perthfhire, fell tragically out with a Yeoman
that liv'd hard by, who coming into a Companie
within ane Ale-houfe, where a Seer fat at Table,
that at the Sight of the Intrant Neighbour, the
Seer ftarting, rofe to go out of the Hous ; and
being afked the Reafon of his haft, told that
the intrant Man fhould die within two Days ;
at which News the named Intrant ftabb'd the
Seer, and was himfelf executed two Days after
for the Faft.

A MINISTER, verie intelligent, but mifbeliev-
ing all fuch Sights as were not ordinar, chance-
ing to be in a narrow Lane with a Seer, who
perceaving a Wight of a known Vifage furioflie
to encounter them, the Seer defired the Minifter
to turn out of the Way; who fcorning his
                                        Reafon

Reafon, and holding him felfe in the Path with them, when the Seer was going haftily out of the Way, they were both violently caft a fide to a good Diftance, and the Fall made them lame for all their Lyfe. A little after the Minifter was carried Home, one came to tol the Bell for the Death of the Man whofe Reprefentation met them in the narrow Path fome Halfe ane Hour before.

ANOTHER Example is : A Seer in Kintyre, in Scotland, fitting at Table with diverfe others, fuddenly did caft his Head afide. The Companie afking him why he did it, he anfwered, that fuch a Friend of his, by Name, then in Ireland, threatened immediately to caft a Difh-full of Butter in his Face. The Men wrote down the Day and Hour, and fent to the Gentleman to know the Truth; which Deed the Gentleman declared he did at that verie Time, for he knew that his Friend was a Seer, and would make fport with it. The Men that were prefent, and examined the Matter exactly, told me this Story; and with all, that a Seer would with all his Opticks perceive no other Object fo readily as this, at fuch a Diftance.

A SUCCINT ACCOMPT

OF

My LORD TARBOTT'S RELATIONS,

IN A LETTER TO THE

HONOURABLE ROBERT BOYLE, ESQUIRE,

OF THE

PREDICTIONS MADE BY SEERS,

Whereof himfelf was Ear and Eye-witnefs.

[I thought fit to adjoyne [it] hereunto, that I
might not be thought fingular in this Dif-
quifition; that the Mater of Fact might
be undenyably made out; and that I
might, with all Submiffion, give Annotations, with Animadverfions, on his fuppofed
Caufes of that Phenomenon, with my
Reafons of Diffent from his Judgement.]

SIR,

I HEARD very much, but beleived very little,
of the Second Sight; yet its being affumed

by

by feverall of great Veracity, I was induced
to make Inquirie after it in the Year 1652,
being then confin'd to abide in the North of
Scotland by the Englifh Ufurpers. The more
generall Accounts of it were, that many Highlanders, yet far more Iflanders, were qualified
with this Second Sight; that Men, Women,
and Children, indiftinctly, were fubject to it,
and Children, where Parents were not. Some
times People came to age, who had it not
when young, nor could any tell by what
Means produced. It is a Trouble to moft of
them who are fubject to it, and they would
be rid of it any Rate if they could. The
Sight is of no long Duration, only continuing
fo long as they can keep their Eyes fteady
without twinkling. The hardy therefore fix
their look, that they may fee the longer; but
the timorous fee only Glances, their Eyes always twinkles at the firft Sight of the Object.
That which generally is feen by them, are the
Species of living Creatures, and of inanimate
Things, which was in Motion, fuch as Ships,
and Habits upon Perfons. They never fie
the

the Species of any Perfon who is already dead. What they foirfie fails not to exift in the Mode, and in that Place where it appears to them. They cannot well know what Space of Time fhall interveen between the Apparition and the real Exiftance: But fome of the hardieft and longeft Experience have fome Rules for Conjectures; as, if they fie a Man with a fhrowding Sheet in the Apparition, they will conjecture at the Nearnefs or Remotenefs of his Death by the more or lefs of his Bodie that is covered by it. They will ordinarily fie their abfent Friends, tho at a great Diftance, fome tymes no lefs than from America to Scotland, fitting, ftanding, or walking in fome certain Place; and then they conclude with a Affurance that they will fie them fo and there. If a Man be in love with a Woman, they will ordinarily fie the Species of that Man ftanding by her, and fo likewife if a Woman be in love; and they conjecture at their Enjoyments (of each other) by the Species touching (of) the Perfon, or appearing at a Diftance from her (if they enjoy not one another.) If they fie the

the Species of any Perſon who is ſick to die, they ſie them covered over with the ſhrowding Sheet.

THESE Generalls I had verified to me by ſuch of them as did ſie, and were eſteemed honeſt and ſober by all the Neighbourhood; for I inquired after ſuch for my Information. And becauſe there were more of theſe Seers in the Iſles of Lewis, Harris, and Uiſt, than in any other Place, I did entreat Sir James M'Donald (who is now dead) Sir Normand M'Loud, and Mr. Daniel Moriſon, a verie honeſt Perſon, (who are ſtill alive,) to make Inquirie in this uncouth Sight, and to acquaint me therewith; which they did, and all found ane Agriement in theſe Generalls, and informed me of many Inſtances confirming what they ſaid. But though Men of Diſcretion and Honour, being but at 2d Hand, I will chooſe rather to put myſelf than my Friends on the Hazard of being laughed at for incredible Relations.

I WAS once travelling in the Highlands, and a good Number of Servants with me, as is uſuall
                                                            there

there ; and one of them going a little before
me, entering into a Houſe where I was to ſtay
all Night, and going haiſtily to the Door, he
ſuddenly ſtept back with a Screech, and did
fall by a Stone, which hit his Foot. I aſked
what the Matter was, for he ſeemed to be very
much frighted. He told me very ſeriouſly
that I ſhould not lodge in that Houſe, becauſe
ſhortly a dead Coffin would be carried out of it,
for many were carrying of it when he was heard
cry. I neglecting his Words, and ſtaying
there, he ſaid to other of his Servants, he was
ſorry for it, and that ſurely what he ſaw would
ſhortly come to paſs. Tho no ſick Perſon was
then there, yet the Landlord, a healthy High-
lander, died of ane appoplectick Fit before I
left the Houſe.

In the year 1653, Alexander Monro (after-
ward Lieut. Coll. to the Earl of Dunbarton's
Regiment,) and I were walking in a Place
called Ullabill, in Lochbroom, on a little Plain,
at the Foot of a rugged Hill. There was a
Servant working with a Spade in the Walk
before us ; his Back was to us, and his Face to
the

the Hill. Before we came to him, he let the
Spade fall, and looked toward the Hill. He
took Notice of us as wee paffed neer by him,
which made me look at him; and perceiving
him to ftair a little ftrangely, I conjectured him
to be a Seer. I called at him, at which he
ftarted and fmiled. What are you doing? faid
I. He anfwered, I have feen a very ftrange
Thing; ane Army of Englifhmen, leeding of
Horfes, coming doun that Hill; and a Number
of them are come down to the Plain, and eating the Barley, which is growing in the Field
neer to the Hill. This was on the 4th May,
(for I notted the Day,) and it was four or fyve
Days before the Barley was fown in the Field
he fpoke of. Alexander Monro afked him how
he knew they were Englifhmen? He faid,
becaufe they were leeding of Horfes, and had
on Hats and Bootts, which he knew no Scot
Man would have there. We took little Notice
of the whole Storie, as other than a foolifh
Vifion; but wifhed that ane Englifh Partie
were there, we being then at Warr with them,
and the Place almoft unacceffable for Horfe-
men

men. But in the Beginning of Auguſt ther-
after, the Earle of Midleton (then Lieut. for
the King in the Highlands) having occaſion to
march a Party of his toward the South Highlands, he ſent his Foot thorow a Place called
Inverlawell; and the Fore-partie which was
firſt down the Hill, did fall off eating the
Barley which was on the litle Plain under it.
And Monro calling to mynd what the Seer told
us, in May preceiding, he wrote of it, and ſent
ane Expreſs to me to Lochſlin, in Roſs, (where
I then was) with it.

I HAD Occaſion once to be in Companie
where a Young Lady was, (excuſe my not
naming of Perſons,) and I was told there was
a notable Seer in the Companie. I called him
to ſpeak with me, as I did ordinarly when I
found any of them ; and after he had anſwered
me to ſeveral Queſtions, I aſked if he knew any
Perſon to be in love with that Lady. He ſaid
he did, but he knew not the Perſon ; for during
the two Dayes he had been in her Company,
he perceaved one ſtanding neer her, and his
Head leaning on her Shoulder ; which he ſaid
did

did fore-tell that the Man fhould marrie her, and die before her, according to his Obferva- tion. This was in the Year 1655. I defired him to defcribe the Perfon, which he did; fo that I could conjecture, by the Defcription, of fuch a one, who was of that Ladyes Acquaint- ance, tho there were no thought of their Mar- riage till two Years thereafter. And having Occafion, in the Year 1657, to find this Seer, who was ane Iflander, in Company with the other Perfon whom I conjectured to have been defcribed by him, I called him afide, and afked if that was the Perfon he faw befide the Lady near two Years then paft. He faid it was he indeed, for he had feen that Lady juft then ftanding by him Hand in Hand. This was fome few Months before their Marriage, and that Man is fince dead, and the Lady ftill alive.

I SHALL trouble you but with one more, which I thought moft remarkable of any that occurred to me. In January 1652, the above mentioned Lieut. Coll. Alex. Monro and I happened to be in the Houfe of one Wm. M'Cleud of Ferrinlea, in the County of Rofs.

He

He, the Landlord, and I were fitting in three Chairs neir the Fire, and in the Corner of the great Chimney there were two Iflanders, who were that verie Night come to the Hous, and were related to the Landlord. While the one of them was talking with Monro, I perceaved the other to look oddly toward me. From this Look, and his being ane Iflander, I conjectured him a Seer, and afked him, at what he ftair'd? He anfwered, by defiring me to rife from that Chair, for it was ane unluckie one. I afked him why. He anfwered, becaufe there was a dead Man in the Chair nixt to me. Well, faid I, if it be in the nixt Chair, I may keep mine own. But what is the Liknefs of the Man? He faid he was a tall Man, with a long Grey Coat, booted, and one of his Legs hanging over the Arme of the Chair, and his head hanging dead to the other Side, and his Arme backward, as if it were brocken. There were fome Englifh Troops then quartered near that Place, and there being at that Time a great Froft after a Thaw, the Country was covered all over with Yce. Four or Fyve of the Englifh ryding by

this

this Houfe fome two Hours after the Vifion, while we were fitting by the Fire, we heard a great Noife, which prov'd to be thofe Troopers, with the Help of other Servants, carrying in one of their Number, who had got a very mif-cheivous Fall, and had his Arme broke; and falling frequently in fwooning Fits, they brought him into the Hall, and fet him in the verie Chair, and in the verie Pofture that the Seer had prophefied. But the Man did not die, though he recovered with great Difficulty.

AMONG the Accounts given me by Sir Nor-mand M'clud, there was one worth of fpecial Notice, which was thus. There [was] a Gentle-man in the Ifle of Harris, who was always feen by the Seers with ane Arrow in his Thigh. Such in the Ifle who thought thofe prognoftica-tions infalliable, did not doubt but he would be fhot in the Thigh before he died. Sir Nor-mand told me that he heard it the Subject of their Difcourfe for many Years. At laft he died without any fuch Accident. Sir Normand was at his Buriall, at St Clement's Church in the Harris. At the fame Time, the Corps of

another

another Gentleman was brought to be buried
in the fame verie Church. The Friends on
either Side came to debate who fhould firft
enter the Church, and in a Trice from Words
they came to Blows. One of the Number (who
was arm'd with Bow and Arrows) let one fly
among them. (Now everie Familie in that Ifle
have their Buriall-place in the Church in Stone
Chefts, and the Bodies are carried in open
Biers to the Buriall-place.) Sir Normand
having appeafed the Tumult, one of the Arrows
was found fhot in the dead Man's Thigh. To
this Sir Normand was a Witnefs.

In the Account which Mr Daniel Morifon,
Parfon in the Lewis, gave me, there was one,
tho it be hetergeneous from the fubject, yet it
may [be] worth your Notice. It was of a
young Woman in his Parifh, who was mightily
frightned by feeing her own Image ftill before
her, alwayes when fhe came to the open Air;
the Back of the Image being alwayes to her,
fo that it was not a reflection as in a Mirrour,
but the Species of fuch a Body as her own, and
in a very like Habit, which appeared to herfelf

D   continually

continually before her. The Parſon keept her
a long whyle with him, but had no Remedy of
her Evill, which troubled her exceidingly. I
was told afterwards, that when ſhe was four or
fyve Years elder ſhe ſaw it not.

THESE are Matters of Faćt, which I aſſure
yow they are truely related. But theſe, and all
others that occurred to me, by Information or
otherwiſe, could never lead me into a remote
Conjećture of the Cauſe of ſo extraordinary a
Phænomenon. Whither it be a Quality in the
Eyes of ſome People into theſe Pairts, concur-
ring with a Quality in the Air alſo; whither
ſuch Species be every where, tho not ſeen by
the Want of Eyes ſo qualified, or from whatever
other Cauſe, I muſt leave to the Inquiry of
clearer Judgements than mine. But a Hint
may be taken from this image which appeared
ſtill to this Woman abovementioned, and from
another mentioned by Ariſtotle, in the 4th of
his Metaphyſicks (if I remember right, for it is
long ſince I read it ;) as alſo from the common
Opinion that young Infants (unſullied with
many Objećts) do ſie Appearitions, which were

not

not feen by thofe of elder Years; as like wife
from this, that feveralls did fie the Second
Sight when in the Highlands or Ifles, yet when
tranfported to live in other Countreys, efpeci-
ally in America, they quite lofe this Qualitie, as
was told me by a Gentleman who knew fome
of them in Barbadoes, who did fee no Vifion
there, altho he knew them to be Seers when
they lived in the Ifles of Scotland.

Thus far my Lord Tarbett.

MY LORD, after narrow Inquifition, hath delivered many true and remarkable obferves
on this Subject; yet to encourage a further
Scrutiny, I crave leave to fay,

THAT 1. But a few Women are endued with
this Sight in refpect of Men, and their Predictions not fo certane.

2. This Sight is not criminal, fince a Man
can come by it unawares, and without his
Confent; but it is certaine he fie more fatall
and fearfull Things than he do gladfome.

3. THE Seers avouch, that feveralls who go

to

to the *Siths*, (or People at Reſt, and, in reſpect
of us, in Peace,) before the natural Period of
their Lyfe expyre, do frequently appear to
them.

4. A VEHEMENT Deſyre to attain this Airt is
very helpfull to the Inquyrer; and the Species
of ane Abſent Friend, which appears to the
Seers, as clearly as if he had ſent his lively
Picture to preſent it ſelfe before him, is no
phantaſtick Shaddow of a ſick Apprehenſion,
but a reality, and a Meſſinger, coming for unknown Reaſons, not from the originall Simi-
litude of it ſelfe, but from a more ſwift and
pragmantick People, which recreat them ſelves
in offering ſecret Intelligence to Men, tho
generally they are unacquainted with that Kind
of Correſpondence, as if they had lived in a
different element from them.

5. THO my Collections were written long
before I ſaw My Lord of Tarbett's, yet I am
glad that his deſcriptions and mine correſpond
ſo nearly. The Maid my Lord mentions, who
ſaw her Image ſtill before her, ſuteth with the
CO-WALKER named in my Account; which tho
                                          ſome

fome, at firft Thought, might conjecture to be
by the Refraction of a Cloud or Mift, as in the
Parelij, (the whole Air and every Drop of
Water being a Mirrour to returne the Species
of Things, were our vifive Faculty fharpe
enough to apprehend them,) or a naturall Reflexion, from the fame Reafons that an Echo
can be redoubled by Airt; yet it were more
fafable to impute this Second Sight to a
Quality infufed into the Eye by ane Unction:
for Witchies have a fleepie Oyntment, that, when
applyed, troubles their Fantafies, advancing it
to have unufuall Figures and Shapes reprefented to it, as if it were a Fit of Fanaticifm,
Hypocondriack Melancholly, or Poffeffion of
fome infinuating Spirit, raifing the Soul beyond
its common Strain, if the palpable Inftances
and Realities feen, and innocently objected to
the Senfes did not difprove it, make the Matter
a palpable Verity, and no Deception; yet fince
this Sight can be beftowed without Oyntment,
or dangerous Compact, the Qualification is not
of fo bad an Originall. Therefore,

6. By my Lord's good Leave, I prefume to
fay

fay, that this Sight can be no Quality of the
Air nor of the Eyes; becaus, 1. such as live
in the fame Air, and fie all other Things as
farr off and as clearly, yet have not the SECOND
SIGHT. 2. A SEER can give another Perfon
this Sight tranfiently, by putting his Hand
and Foot in the Pofture he requires of him.
3. The unfullied Eyes of Infants can naturally
perceave no new unaccuftomed Objects, but
what appear to other Men, unlefs exalted
and clarified fome Way, as Ballaam's Afs for a
Time; tho in a Witches Eye the Beholder
cannot fie his own Image reflected, as in the
Eyes of other People; fo that Defect of Objects, as well as Diverfities of the Subject,
may appear differently on feverall Tempers
and Ages. 4. Tho alfo fome are of fo vene-
mous a Conftitution, by being radicated in
Envy and Malice, that they pierce and kill
(like a Cockatrice) whatever Creature they firft
fet their Eye on in the Morning; fo was it
with Walter Grahame, fome Time living in
the Paroch wherein now I am, who killed his
own Cow after commending its Fatnefs, and
                                        fhot

ſhot a Hair with his Eyes, having praiſed its ſwiftneſs, (ſuch was the Infection of ane evill Eye;) albeit this was unuſuall, yet he ſaw no Object but what was obvious to other Men as well as to himſelfe. 5. If the being tranſported to live in another Countrey did obſcure the Second Sight, nather the Parſon nor the Maid needed be much troubled for her Reflexſelfe; a little Peregrination, and going from her wonted Home, would have ſalved her Fear. Wherefore,

7. SINCE the Things ſeen by the Seers are real Entities, the Preſages and Predictions found true, but a few endued with this Sight, and thoſe not of bad Lyves, or addicted to Malifices, the true Solution of the Phænomenon ſeems rather to be, the courteous Endeavours of our fellow Creatures in the Inviſible World to convince us, (in Oppoſition to Sadduce's, Socinians, and Atheiſts,) of a Deity; of Spirits; of a poſſible and harmleſs Method of Correſpondence betwixt Men and them, even in this Lyfe; of their Operation for our Caution and Warning; of the Orders and Degrees

of

of Angells, whereof one Order, with Bodies of
Air condenfed and curioufly fhap't, may be nixt
to Man, fuperior to him in Underftanding, yet
unconfirmed ; and of their Region, Habitation,
and Influences on Man, greater than that of
Starrs on inanimat Bodies ; a Knowledge (be-
like) referved for thefe laft atheiftick Ages,
wherein the Profanity of Mens Lives hath de-
bauched and blinded their Underftanding, as
to MOSES, JESUS, and the Prophets, (unlefs
they get Convictions from Things formerly
known,) as from the Regions of the Dead :
nor doth the ceafing of the Vifions, upon the
Seers Tranfmigration into forrein Kingdoms,
make his Lordfhip's Conjecture of the Quality
of the Air and Eye a white the more probable ; but, on the Contrary, it confirms greatly
my Account of ane Invifible People, guardian
over and care-full of Men, who have their
different Offices and Abilities in diftinct Coun-
terey's, as appears in Dan. 10. 13. viz. about
Ifraels, Grecia's, and Perfia's affiftant Princes,
whereof who fo prevaileth giveth Dominion
and Afcendant to his Pupills and Vaffalls over
the

the oppofite Armies and Countreys; fo that
every Countrey and Kingdom having their
topical Spirits, or Powers affifting and govern-
ing them, the SCOTTISH SEER banifhed to
America, being a Stranger there, as well to
the invifible as to the vifible Inhabitants, and
wanting a Fimiliarity of his former Correfpon-
dents, he could not have the Favour and
Warnings, by the feverall Vifions and Predictions which were wont to be granted him by
thefe Acquantances and Favourites in his own
Countrey. For if what he wont to fie were
Realities, (as I have made appear,) 'twere too
great ane Honour for Scotland to have fuch
feldom-feen Watchers and predominant Powers
over it alone, acting in it fo expreffly, and all
other Nations wholly deftitute of the lyke;
tho, without all peradventure, all other People
wanted the right Key of their Cabinet, and
the exact Method of Correfpondence with them,
except the fagacious active Scots, as many of
them have retained it of a long Time, and by
Surpryfes and Raptures do often foirtell what
in Kyndnefs is really reprefented to them at
feverall

feverall Occafions. To which Purpofe the learned lynx-ey'd Mr. Baxter, on Rev. 12. 7. writting of the Fight betwixt Michaell and the Dragon, gives a verie pertinent Note, viz. That he knows not but ere any great Action (efpeciall tragicall) is don on Earth, that firft the Battell and Victory is acted and atchieved in the Air betwixt the good and evill Spirits : Thus he. It feems thefe were the mens Guardians; and the lyke Battells are oft tymes perceav'd in a Loaft in the Nycht-time; the Event of which myght eafily be reprefented by fome one of the Number to a Correfpondent on Earth, as frequently the Report of great Actions have been more fwiftly caried to other Countreys than all the Airt of us Mortals could poffibly difpatch it. St. Auftine, on Mark, 9. 4. giveth no fmall Intimation of this Truth, averring that Elias appeared with Jefus on the Mount in his proper Bodie, but Mofes in ane aereall Bodie, affumed like the Angels who appeared, and had Ability to eat with Abraham, tho no Neceffity on the Account of their Bodies. As lyke wife the late Doctrine of the Pre-exiftence

of

of Souls, living into aereall Vehicles, gives a fingular Hint of the Poffibility of the Thing, if not a direct Prooff of the whole Affertion; which yet moreover may be illuminated by diverfe other Inftances of the lyke Nature, and as wonderfull, befides what is above faid. As,

8. THE invifible Wights which haunt Houfes feem rather to be fome of our fubterranean Inhabitants, (which appear often to Men of the Second Sight,) than evill Spirits or Devills; becaufe, tho they throw great Stones, Pieces of Earth and Wood, at the Inhabitants, they hurt them not at all, as if they acted not malitioufly, like Devills at all, but in Sport, lyke Buffoons and Drolls. All Ages have affoorded fome obfcure Teftimonies of it, as Pythagoras his Doctrine of Tranfmigration; Socrates's Dæmon that gave him [Warning] of future Dangers; Platoe's claffing them into various vehiculated Speciefes of Spirits; Dionifius Areopagita's marfhalling nyne Orders of Spirits, fuperiour and fubordinate; the Poets their borrowing of the Philofophers, and add-
ing

ing their own Fancies of Fountain, River, and
Sea Nymphs, Wood, Hill, and Montain Inhabitants, and that every Place and Thing,
in Cities and Countreys, had fpeciall invifible
regular Gods and Governours. Cardan fpeaks
of his Father his feeing the Species of his
Friend, in a moon-fhyn Night, riding fiercely
by his Window on a white Horfe, the verie
Night his Friend dy'd at a Vaft Diftance from
him; by which he underftood that fome Alteration would fuddenly enfue. Cornelius Aggrippa,
and the learned Dr. Mor, have feverall Paffages tending that Way. The Noctambulo's
themfelves would appear to have fome forrein
joquing Spirit poffeffing and fupporting them,
when they walk on deep Waters and Topes
of Houfes without Danger, when afleep and
in the dark; for it was no way probable that
their Apprehenfion, and ftrong Imagination
fetting the Animal Spirits a work to move the
Body, could preferve it from finking in the
Deepth, or falling down head-long, when afleep,
any more than when awake, the Body being
then as ponderous as before; and it is hard
to

to attribute it to a Spirit flatelie evill and
Enemy to Man, becaufe the Noctambulo returns to his own Place fafe. And the moft
furious Tribe of the Dæmons are not per-
mitted by Providence to attacke Men fo frequently either by Night or by Day: For in
our Highlands, as there may be many fair
Ladies of this aereal Order, which do often
tryft with lafcivious young Men, in the quality
of Succubi, or lightfome Paramours and Strum-
pets, called *Leannain Sith*, or familiar Spirits
(in Dewter. 18. 11.); fo do many of our
Hyghlanders, as if a ftrangling by the Night
MARE, preffed with a fearfull Dream, or rather
poffeffed by one of our aereall Neighbours, rife
up fierce in the Night, and apprehending the
neereft Weapons, do pufh and thruft at all
Perfons in the fame Room with them, fome-
tymes wounding their own Comerades to dead.
The lyke whereof fell fadly out within a few
Miles of me at the writting hereof. I add
but one Inftance more, of a very young Maid,
who lived neir to my laft Refidence, that in
one Night learned a large Peice of Poefy, by
the

the frequent Repetition of it, from one of our nimble and courteous Spirits, whereof a Part was pious, the reſt ſuperſtitious, (for I have a Copy of it,) and no other Perſon was ever heard to repeat it before, nor was the Maid capable to compoſe it of herſelf.

9. He demonſtrated and made evident to Senſe this extraordinary Viſion of our Tramontain Seers, and what is ſeen by them, by what is ſaid above, many haveing ſeen this ſame Spectres and Apparitions at once, haveing their viſive Faculties entire ; for *non eſt diſputandum de guſtu.* Itt now remaines to ſhew that it is not unſutable to Reaſon nor the Holy Scriptures.

First, That it is not repugnant to Reaſon, doeth appear from this, that it is no leſs ſtrange for Immortal Sparks and Souls to come and be immerſed into groſs terreſtrial elementary Bodies, and be ſo propagated, ſo nouriſhed, ſo fed, ſoe cloathed as they are, and breathe in ſuch ane Air and World prepared for them, then for Hollanders or Hollow-cavern Inhabitants to live and traffick among us, in another

State

State of Being, without our Knowledge. For
Raymond de Subinde, in his 3d Booke, Chap.
12. argues quaintly, that all Sorts of Living
Creatures have a happie rational Politie of
· there own, with great Contentment; which
Government and mutual Converfe of theirs
they all pride and pluim themfelves, becaufe
it is as unknown to Man, as Man is to them.
Much more, that the Sone of the HIGHEST
SPIRIT fhould affume a Bodie like ours, con-
vinces all the World that no other Thing that
is poffible needs be much wondered at.

2. The Manucodiata, or Bird of Paradife,
living in the higheft Region of the Air; com-
mon Birds in the fecond Region; Flies and
Infects in the loweft; Men and Beafts on the
Earth's Surface; Worms, Otters, Badgers, in
Waters; lyke wife Hell is inhabited at the
Centre, and Heaven in the Circumference:
can we then think the middle Cavities of the
Earth emptie? I have feen in Weems, (a
Place in the Countie of Fyfe, in Scotland,)
divers Caves cut out as vaft Temples under
Ground; the lyke is a Countie of England;
in

in Malta is a Cave, wherein Stons of a curious Cut are thrown in great Numbers every Day; fo I have had barbed Arrow-heads of yellow Flint, that could not be cut fo fmall and neat, of fo brittle a Subftance, by all the Airt of Man. It would feem therefoir that thefe mention'd Works were done by certaine Spirits of pure Organs, and not by Devills, whofe continual Torments could not allow them fo much Leafure. Befides thefe, I have found fyve Curiofities in Scotland, not much obferv'd to be elfewhere. 1. The Brounies, who in fome Families are Drudges, clean the Houfes and Difhes after all go to Bed, taking with him his Portion of Food and removing befor Day-break. 2. The Mafon Word, which tho fome make a Mifterie of it, I will not conceal a little of what I know. It is lyke a Rabbinical Tradition, in way of Comment on Jachin and Boaz, the two Pillars erećted in Solomon's Temple, (1 Kings, 7. 21.) with ane Addition of fome fecret Signe delyvered from Hand to Hand, by which they know and become familiar one with another. 3. This Second
Sight

Sight, fo largely treated of before. 4. Charmes, and curing by them very many Difeafes, fome-times by transferring the Sicknes to another. 5. A being Proof of Lead, Iron, and Silver, or a Brieve making Men invulnerable. Divers of our Scottifh Commanders and Souldiers have been feen with blue Markes only, after they were fhot with leaden Balls; which feems to be an Italian Trick, for they feem to be a People too currious and magically inclyned. Finally Iris-men, our Northern-Scotifh, and our Athole Men are fo much addicted to and delighted with Harps and Mufick, as if, like King Saul, they were poffeffed with a forrein Spirit, only with this Difference, that Mufick did put Saul's Pley-fellow a fleep, but roufed and awaked our Men, vanquifhing their own Spirits at Pleafure, as if they were impotent of its Powers, and unable to command it; for wee have feen fome poor Beggers of them, chattering their Teeth for Cold, that how foon they faw the Fire, and heard the Harp, leapt thorow the Houfe like Goats and Satyrs. As there paralell Stories in all Countries and Ages

E   reported

reported of thefe our obfcure People, (which are no Dotages,) fo is it no more of Neceffitie to us fully to know their Beings and Manner of Life, then to underftand diftinctly the Politie of the nyne Orders of Angels; or with what Oyl the Lamp of the Sun is maintained fo long and regularlie; or why the Moon is called a great Luminary in Scripture, while it only appears to be fo; or if the Moon be truly inhabited, becaufe Telefcopes difcover Seas and Mountains in it, as well as flaming Fur- nifhes in the Sun; or why the Difcovery of America was look't on as a Fairie Tale, and the Reporters hooted at as Inventors of ridi- culous Utopias, or the firft probable Afferters punifhed as Inventures of new Gods and Worlds; or why in England the King cures the Struma by ftroaking, and the Seventh Son in Scotland; whither his temperat Complexion conveys a Balfome, and fucks out the corrupt- ing Principles by a frequent warme fanative Contact, or whither the Parents of the Seventh Child put furth a more eminent Virtue to his Production than to all the Reft, as being the

certain

certain Meridian and hight to which their
Vigour afcends, and from that furth have a
graduall declyning into a feeblenefs of the
Bodie and its Produ&ion. And then, 1. Why
is not the 7th Son infe&ed himfelfe by that
Contagion he extra&s from another? 2. How
can continual ftroaking with a cold Hand have
foe ftrong a natural Operation, as to exhale
all the Infe&ions warming corroding Vapours.
3. Why may not a 7th Daughter have the
fame Vertue? So that it appears, albeit, a
happie natural Conftitution concurre, yet fomething in it above Nature. Therefore every
Age hath left fome fecret for its Difcoverie;
who knows but this Entercourfe bewixt the
two Kinds of rationall Inhabitants of the fame
Earth may be not only beleived fhortly, but
as friely entertain'd, and as well known, as
now the Airt of Navigation, Printing, Limning,
riding on Saddles with Stirrups, and the Difcoveries of Microfcopes, which were fometimes
a great a Wonder, and as hard to be beleived.

10. Tho I will not be fo curious nor fo
peremptorie as he who will prove the Pofi-
                                        bility

bility of the Philofopher's Stone from Scripture, Job, 28. 1. 2. Job, 22. 24. 25.; or the
Pluralitie of Worlds, from John, 14. 2. and
Hebrews ij. 3.; nor the Circulation of Blood
from Eccles. 12. and 6.; nor the Tanifmanical
Airt, from the Blind and Lame mentioned
in 2d of Samuel, 5. 6. yet I humblie propofe
thefe Paffages which may give fome Light to
our Subject at leaft, and fhow that this Polity
and Rank of People is not a Thing impoffible,
nor the modeft and innocent Scrutiny of them
impertinent or unfafe. The Legion or Brigad
of Spirits (mentioned Mark, 5. 10.) befought
our Saviour not to fend them away out of the
Countrey; which fhows they were DÆMONES
LOCI, Topical Spirits, and peculiar Superin-
tendents and Supervifors affign'd to that Province. And the Power over the Nations
granted (Rev. 2. 26.) to the Conquerors of
Vice and Infidelitie, Sound fomewhat to that
Purpofe. Tobit had a Dæmon attending
Marriage, Chap. 6. Verfe, 15; and in Matth.
4. and 5. ane evill Spirit came in a Vifible
Shape to tempt our Saviour, who himfelfe
                                        denyed

denyed not the fenfible appearing of Ghofts to our Sight, but faid, their Bodies were not compofed of Flefh and Bones, as ours, Luke, 24. 39. And in Philip. 2. 10. our verie Sub-terraneans are expreffly faid to bow to the Name of JESUS. Elifha, not intelleCtually only, but fenfibly, faw Gehazi when out of the Reach of ane ordinary View. It wants not good Evidents that there are more managed by God's Spirits, good, evill, and intermediate Spirits, among Men in this World, then we are aware of; the good Spirits ingefting fair and heroick Apprehenfions and Images of Vertue and the divyne Life, thereby animating us to aCt for a higher Happines, according to our Improvement; and relinquifhing us as ftrangely upon our NegleCt, or our embrace-ing the deceatfull fyrene-like PiCtures and Re-prefentations of Pleafures and Gain, prefented to our Imaginations by evill and fportfull Angells, to allure to ane unthinking, ungene-rous, and fenfual Lyfe; non of them having power to compell us to any Mifdemeanour without our flat Confent. Moreover, this Life

of

of ours being called a Warfair, and God's fay-
ing that at laft there will be no Peace to the
Wicked, our buffie and filent Companions alfo
being called *Siths*, or *People at Reft and Quiet*,
in refpeét of us; and withall many Ghofts
appearing to Men that want this *Second Sight*,
in the very Shapes, and fpeaking the fame
Language, they did when incorporate and alive
with us; a Matter that is of ane old impre-
fcriptible Tradition, (*our Highlanders* making
ftill a Diftinétion betwixt *Sluagh Saoghalta*
and *Sluagh Sith*, averring that the Souls goe
to the *Sith* when diflodged;) many real Trea-
fures and Murders being difcovered by Souls
that pafs from among our felves, or by the
Kindnefs of thefe our airie Neighbours, non
of which Spirits can be altogither inorganical.
No lefs than the Confeits about Purgatory, or
a State of Refcue; the *Limbus Patrum et Infan-
tum*, Inventions, [which] tho mifapplyed, yet
are not Chimæras, and altogither groundlefs.
For *ab origine*, it is nothing but blanfh and
faint Difcoveries of this SECRET REPUBLICK of
ours here treated on, and additional Fiétions
of

of Monks doting and crazied Heads, our Creed
saying that our Saviour defcended εἰς ᾅδου, to the
invifible Place and People. And many Divines
fuppofing that the Deity appear'd in a vifible
Shape feen by Adam in the Cooll of the Day,
and fpeaking to him with ane audible voice.
And Jefus, probably by the Miniftery of invifible Attendants, conveying more meat of the
fame Kind to the fyve Thowfand that wes fed
by him with a very few Loaves and Fifhes,
(for a new Creation it was not.) The Zijm-
jiim and Ochim, in Ifa. 13. 21. 22. Thes
Satyres, and doolfull unknown Creatures of
Iflands and Deferts, feem to have a plain Pro-
fpect that Way. Finally, the eternal Happi-
nefs enjoyed in the 3d Heavens, being more
myfterious than moft of Men take it to be.
It is not a fenfe whollie adduced to Scripture
to fay, that this SIGHT, and the due Objects
of it, hath fome Veftige in holy Write, but
rather 'tis modeftly deduced from it.

11. It only now remains to anfear the obvious
Objections againft the Reality and Lawfullnefs
of this Speculation.

Queftion

QUESTION 1. How do you falve the Second Sight from Compact and Witchcraft?

ANSWER. Tho this Correfpondence with the Intermediate Unconfirm'd People (betwixt Man and Angell) be not ordinary to all of us who are Superterraneans, yet this SIGHT falling fome Perfons by Accident, and its being connatural to others from their Birth, the Derivation of it cannot always be wicked. A too great Curio-fitie, indeed, to acquyre any unneceffary Airt, may be blameworthy; but diverfe of the SECRET COMMONWEALTH may, by Permiffion, difcover themfelves as innocently to us, who are in another State, as fome of us Men do to Fifhes, which are in another Element, when we plunge and dive into the Bottom of the Seas, their native Region; and in Procefs of Time we may come to converfe as familiarly with thefe nimble and agile Clans (but with greater Plea-fure and Profit,) as we do now with the Chino's Antipodes.

QUESTION 2. Are they fubject to Vice, Lusts? Paffion, and Injuftice, as we who live on the Surface of the Earth?

Anfwer

ANSWER. The Seers tell us that thefe wandering Aereal People have not fuch an Impetus and fatall Tendency to any Vice as Men, as not being drenched into fo grofs and dregy Bodies as we, but yet are in ane imperfect State, and fome of them making better Effays for heroick Actions than others; having the fame Meafures of Vertue and Vice as wee, and ftill expecting advancement to a higher and more fplendid State of Lyfe. One of them is ftronger than many Men, yet do not incline to hurt Mankind, except by Commiffion for a grofs Mifdemeanour, as the deftroying Angell of Ægypt, and the Affyrians, Exod. 12. 29. 2 Kings, 10. 35. They haunt moft where is moft Barbaritie; and therefoir our ignorant Anceftors, to prevent the Infults of that ftrange People, ufed as rude and courfe a Remedie; fuch as Exorcifms, Donations, and Vows: But how foon ever the true Piety prevailed in any Place, it did not put the Inhabitants beyond the Reach and Awthoritie of thefe fubtile inferiour Co-inhabitants and Colleagues of ours: The FATHER OF ALL SPIRITS, and the Perfon himfelfe

himfelfe, having the only Command of his Soul
and Actions, a concurrance they may have to
what is virtuously done; for upon committing
of a foul Deed, one will find a Demure upon
his Soul, as if his cheerfull Collegue had de-
ferted him.

QUESTION 3. Do thefe airie Tribes procreate? If fo, how are they nourifhed, and at
what period of Time do they die?

ANSWER. Suppofing all Spirits to be created
at once in the Beginning, Souls to pre-exist and
to circle about into feveral States of Probation-
fhip; to make them either totally unexcufable,
or perfectly happie againft the laft Day, folves
all the Difficulties. But in very Deed, and
fpeaking futeable to the Nature of Things, there
is no more Abfurditie for a Spirit to inform ane
Infant in Bodie of Airs, than a Bodie compofed
of dull and drufie Earth; the beft of Spirits
have alwayes delyghted more to appear into
aereal, than into terreftrial Bodyes. They feed
moft what on Quinteffences, and aetheriall
Effences. The Pith and Spirits only of
Women's Milk feed their Children, being arti-
ficially

ficially conveyed, (as Air and Oyl fink into our Bodies,) to make them vigorous and frefh. And this fhorter Way of conveying a pure Aliment, (without the ufuall Digeftions,) by tranffufing it, and tranfpyring thorow the Pores into the Veins, Arteries, and Veffells that fupplie the Bodie, is nothing more abfurd, than ane Infant's being fed by the Navel before it is borne, or than a Plant, which groweth by attracting a livelie Juice from the Earth thorow many fmall Roots and Tendons, whose courfer Pairts be adapted and made connatural to the Whole, doth quickly coalefce by the ambient Cold ; and fo are condenf'd and bak'd up into a confirm'd Wood in the one, and folid Bodie of the Flefh and Bone in the other.   A Notion which, if intertained and approv'd, may fhew that the late Invention of foaking and tranffufing (not Blood, but) athereal virtuall Spirits, may be ufefull both for Nourifhment and Health, whereof is a Veftige in the damnable Practife of evill Angells, their fucking of Blood and Spirits out of Witches Bodys (till they drew them into a deform'd and dry Leannefs,) to feid their own
Vehicles

Vehicles withall, leaving what we call the
Witches Mark behind; a Spot that I have
feen, as a fmall Mole, horny, and brown-
coloured; throw which Mark, when a large
Brafs Pin was thruft (both in Buttock, Nofe,
and Rooff of the Mouth,) till it bowed and
become crooked, the Witches, both Men and
Women, nather felt a Pain, nor did bleed, nor
knew the precife Time when this was adoing to
them, (there Eyes only being covered.) Now
the Air being a Body as well as Earth, no
Reafon can be given why there may not be
Particles of more vivific Spirit form'd of it for
Procreation, then is poffible to be of Earth,
which takes more Time and Pains to rarify and
ripen it, ere it can come to have a prolific
Virtue. And if our Aping Darlings did not
thus procreate, there whole Number would be
exhaufted after a confiderable Space of Time.
For tho they are of more refyned Bodies and
Intellectualls than wee, and of far lefs heavy
and corruptive Humours, (which caufe a Dif-
folution,) yet many of their Lives being dif-
fonant to right Reafon and their own Laws,
                                                    and

and their Vehicles not being wholly frie of Luſt
and Paſſion, eſpecially of the more ſpirituall
and hautie Sins they paſs (after a long healthy
Lyfe) into one Orb and Receptacle fitted for
their Degree, till they come under the general
Cognizance of the laſt Day.

QUESTION 4. Doth the acquiring of this
Second Sight make any Change on the Ac-
quirers Body, Mind, or Actions?

ANSWER. All uncouth SIGHTS enfeebles the
SEER. Daniel, tho familiar with divyne Viſions,
yet fell frequently doun without Strength, when
dazzled with a Power which had the Aſcendant
of, and paſſed on him beyond his Comprehen-
ſion, Chap. 10. 8. 17. So our SEER is put in
a Rapture, Tranſport, and ſort of Death, as
diveſted of his Body and all its Senſes, when
he is firſt made participant of this curious
Peice of Knowledge : But it maketh no Wramp
or Strain in the Underſtanding of any ; only to
the Fancy's of clownish or illiterate Men, it
creates ſome Affrightments and Diſturbances,
becauſe of the Strongneſs of the Showes, and
their Unacquaintedneſs with them. And as for
their

their Lyfe, the Perfons endued with this Rarity
are, for the moſt Part, candid, honeſt, and
ſociable People. If any of them be ſubjeƈt to
Immoralities, this obſtruſe Skill is not to be
blamed for it; for unleſs themſelves be the
Tempters, the Colonies of the Inviſible Planta-
tions, with which they intercommune, do pro-
voke them by no Villainy or Malifice, nather
at their firſt Acquaintance nor after a long
Familiarity.

QUESTION 5. Doth not Sathan interpoſe in
ſuch Caſes by many ſubtile unthought Inſinua-
tions, as to him who let the Fly, or Familiar,
go out of the Box, and yet found the Fly of his
own putting in, as ſerviceable as the other
would have been?

ANSWER. The Goodneſs of the Lyfe, and
Deſigns of the ancient Prophets and Seers, was
one of the beſt Prooffs of their Miſſion.[1]

---

[1] The original Transcriber has added:
"See the Rest in a little Manuscript belonging to Coline
Kirk," probably the author's son of that name.—A. L.

NOTE.

IN trying to collect evidence as to the Rerrick "evil spirit" from Kirk-Session Records, I have been most kindly assisted by the Rev. Mr. M'Conachie, Minister of Rerrick. Mr. M'Conachie finds that only two parishes in the Stewartry, Kells and Girthon, have records containing the years 1695, 1696. The records of Rerrick do not go so far back. We are therefore left to the pamphlet of 1696, by Telfair, which is an unusually business-like statement, the names of attesting witnesses being added in the marginal notes. For phenomena singularly similar to those of Rerrick, *Obeah*, by Mr. H. J. Bell, may be consulted. (*Obeah*, Sampson Low & Co., London, 1889, p. 93.)

NOTES.

INTRODUCTION.

Note (*a*), p. xvi.—"The Psychical Society."

The Psychical Society, as far as the writer is aware, has not examined officially the old accounts of the phenomena which it investigates at present. The Catalogue of the Society's Library, however, proves that it does not lack the materials.

Note (*b*), p. xxx.—"Their speech is a kind of whistling."

That the voice of spirits is a kind of whistling, twittering, or chirping, is a very widely diffused and ancient belief. The ghosts in Homer twitter like bats; in New Caledonia an English settler found that he could scare the natives from a piece of ground by whistling there at night. Mr. Samuel Wesley says, "I followed the noise into almost every room in the house, both by day and by night, with lights and without, and have sat alone for some time, and, when I heard the noise, spoke to it to tell me what it was, but never heard any articulate voice, and only once or twice two or three feeble squeaks, a little louder than the chirping of a bird, and not like the noise of rats, which I have often heard" (*Memoirs of the Wesley Family*, p. 164). Professor Alexander mentions the "pecular whistling sound" at some manifestations in Rio Janeiro as "rather frequent" (*Proc. S. P. R.,*

xix. 180). Here children were the mediums ; how did
they get the idea of the traditional whistle ? See also
the following note.

Note (c), p. xl.—"Not long after the Spanish conquest
of Peru."

The phenomena alluded to here are said to have
occurred in 1549. The evidence is a mere report by
Cieza de Leon, who does not pretend to have been an
eye-witness. But, as Mr. Clements Markham, Cieza's
editor, remarks, the phenomena are analogous to those
of spiritualism. At the very least, we find a belief in
this kind of manifestation at a remote date, and in an
outlandish place. Cieza says : [1]

"When the Adelantado Belalcazar was governor of
the province of Popyan, and when Gomez Hernandez
was his lieutenant in the town of Auzerma, there was a
chief in a village called Pirsa, almost four leagues from
the town, whose brother, a good-looking youth named
Tamaraqunga, inspired by God, wished to go to the
town of the Christians to receive baptism. But the
devils did not wish that he should attain his desire,
fearing to lose what seemed secure, so they frightened
this Tamaraqunga in such sort that he was unable to do
anything. God permitting it, the devils stationed themselves in a place where the chief alone could see them,
in the shape of birds called *auras.* Finding himself so
persecuted by the devils, he sent in great haste to a
Christian living near, who came at once, and hearing
what he wanted, signed him with the sign of the cross.
But the devils then frightened him more than ever,
appearing in hideous forms, which only were visible to

---

[1] *The Travels of Pedro de Cieza de Leon,* ch. cxviii.

him. *The Christian only saw stones falling from the air and heard whistling.* A brother of one Juan Pacheco, citizen of the same town, then holding office in the place of Gomez Hernandez, who had gone to Caramanta, came from Auzerma with another man to visit the Indian chief. They say that Tamaraqunga was much frightened and ill-treated by the devils, who carried him through the air from one place to another in presence of the Christians, he complaining and the devils whistling and shouting. Sometimes when the chief was sitting with a glass of liquor before him, the Christians saw the glass raised up in the air and put down empty, and a short time afterwards the wine was again poured into the cup from the air." Compare what Ibn Batuta, the old Arab traveller, saw at the court of the King of Delhi. The matter is discussed in Colonel Yule's *Marco Polo.*

This may suffice as a specimen of the manifestations. They continued while the chief was on his way to church ; he was lifted into the air, and the Christians had to hold him down. In church the ghostly whistling was heard, and stones fell around, while the chief said that he saw devils standing upside down, and himself was thrown into that unusual posture. The combination of convulsive movements with the other phenomena is that which we have already remarked in the cases of " Mr. H." and the grandson of William Morse. Cieza de Leon says that the chief was not troubled after his baptism. The illusions of the newly-converted, so like those of the early Christian hermits, are described by Callaway in his *Zulu Tales.*

Note (d), p. 1.

Priestley's explanation of the Epworth disturbances is imposture by the servants, by way of a practical joke.

Coleridge, on the other hand, says that "all these stories, and I could produce fifty cases at least equally well authenticated, and, as far as the veracity of the narrators, and the single fact of their having seen and heard such and such sights or sounds, above all rational scepticism, are as much like one another as the symptoms of the same disease in different patients."

It is a pity that Coleridge did not produce his fifty well-authenticated examples. The similarity of the narratives everywhere, all the world over, is exactly what makes them interesting. Coleridge goes on: 'This indeed I take to be the true and only solution—a contagious nervous disease, the acme, or intensest form of which is catalepsy" (Southey's *Wesley*, vol. i. p. 14, Coleridge's note). If there be such a contagious nervous disease, it is a very remarkable malady, and well worth examining. The Wesleys were not alarmed ; they bantered the spirit ; they wished they could set him to work ; and beyond the trembling of the children when Jeffrey was knocking during their sleep, there is no sign of morbid conditions. A neighbouring clergyman, who was asked to pass a night in the house, saw and heard just what the others heard and saw.[1] The hypothesis of a contagious nervous disease, in which every witness exhibits the same symptoms of illusion in all parts of the world, is a theory which needs a good deal of verification. Where material traces of the disturbances remain, it is absurd to speak of contagious hallucinations. We must fall back on the hypothesis of trickery, or must say with Southey, "Such things may be preternatural, yet not miraculous ; they may not be in the ordinary course of nature, yet imply no alteration of its laws." Any theory is more plausible than the idea that Mr. Wesley and Mr. Hoole

---

[1] Mr. Hoole's account, *Memoirs of the Wesleys*, p. 91.

were in a state bordering on catalepsy. Believers in hypnotism may think it possible that this, that, and the other persons, if they submitted themselves to hypnotic influences, might have the same hallucinations suggested to them. But there is no evidence, in the Epworth case nor in the Rerrick case, of any such matter. "So far as we yet know, sensory hallucination of several persons together, *who are not in a hypnotic state*, is a rare phenomenon, and therefore not a probable explanation" (*Proc. S. P. R.*, iv. 62). There is some evidence that epileptic patients suffer from the same illusions —for example, the presence of a woman in a red cloak; and in *delirium tremens* the "horrors" are usually similar. But that all the persons who enter a given house should be impressed by the same material illusions, as of chairs and tables, and even beds (like Nancy Wesley's) flying about, is a theory more incredible than the hypothesis either of trickery or of abnormal occurrences. When the disturbances always cease on the arrival of a competent witness, then it is not hard to say which theory we ought to choose. For imposture see next note.

Note (e), p. lvii.—"Children at *séances.*"

The phenomena discussed are most frequently connected with children, who may be regarded either as mediums or impostors, conscious or unconscious. In *Proc. S. P. R.*, iv. 25-42, Professor Barrett gives the case of a little girl whom he knew. She had raps wherever she went, even when alone with the Professor, who made her stand with her hands against the wall, at the greatest stretch of her arms, "with the muscles of the legs and arms all in tension." "A brisk pattering of raps" followed Professor Barrett's request. But he also mentions a boy "of juvenile piety," who "for twelve months deceived his father, a distinguished surgeon, and all his family, by pretended spiritualistic manifestations, which appeared at first sight inexplicable, until the cunning trickery of the lad was discovered." The only difference between these cases is that an "outsider" discovered trickery in one instance and not in the other. This is a very ticklish kind of certainty, and it is plain that children can do a great deal in the way of mere imposture. The state of any young Wesley who might have been caught out is unenviable. Verily Mr. Wesley would not have spared for his crying.

Note (f), p. lxii.—"The pricking of witches."

It is pretty certain that some of these unlucky old women were pricked "in anæsthetic areas."

Note (a), p. 8.—"These Arrows that fly in the Dark."

The arrows are the ancient flint arrow-heads, which Mr. Kirk later asserts to be too delicate for human artificers. On this matter Isabel Gowdie, the witch, confessed, "As for Elf arrows, the Divell sharpes them with his ain hand, and deliveris them to Elf boys, wha whyttlis and dightis them with a sharp thing lyk a paking needle; bot whan I was in Elfland, I saw them whyttling and dighting them." Isabel described the manner in which witches use this artillery: "We spang them from the naillis of our thoombs," and with these she and her friends shot and slew many men and women. The confessions of Isabel Gowdie are in the third volume of Pitcairn's *Scottish Criminal Trials.* They contain little or nothing of the "psychical;" all is mere folk-lore, fairy tales, and charms derived from the old Catholic liturgy. The poor woman, having begun to fable, fabled

with manifest enjoyment and considerable power. It
seems from her account that each "Covin," or assembly
of witches, had a maiden in it, and "without our maiden
we could do no great thing." On the other hand, an
extraordinary case of an epileptic boy, who was hurled
about, and beheld distant occurrences in trance, may be
read in Chambers's *Domestic Annals of Scotland*, iii. 449.
Candles used to go out when this boy, a third son of
Lord Torpichen, was in the room. The date (1720) and
the place (Mid-Lothian) prevented any one from being
burned for bewitching him. A fast was proclaimed.
The boy recovered, and did good service in the navy.
He is said to have been "levitated" frequently."

Note (b), p. 11.—"Milk thorow a hair-tedder."

Isabel Gowdie confessed to stealing milk from the
cow by magic. "We plait the rope the wrong way, in
the Devil's name, and we draw the tether between the
cow's hind feet, and out betwixt her forward feet, in the
Devil's name, and thereby take with us the cow's milk."

Mr. Kirk, it will be observed, does not connect the
Fairy kingdom with that of Satan, as some of his con-
temporaries were inclined to do.

Note (c), p. 19.—"The Wreath (wraith) . . . is only
    exuvious fumes of the Man, . . . exhaled and con-
    gealed into a various likeness."

What is this theory of "Men illiterate and unwary in
their Observations," but Von Hartmann's doctrine of
"the nerve force which issues from the body of the
medium, and then proceeds to set up fresh centres of
force in all neighbouring objects . . . while it still
remains under the control of the medium's unconscious
will"? See Mr. Walter Leaf on Hartmann's *Der
Geisterhypothese des Spiritismus, Proc. S. P. R.,* xix. 293.

It is amusing to find a learned German coinciding in scientific theory with "ignorant and unwary" Highland seers. Both regard the phantasms as manifestations of "nerve-force," "exuvious fumes," and as "neither souls nor counterfeiting spirits."

Note (d), p. 23.—"Fairy hills."

The hypothesis that the Fairy belief may be a tradition of an ancient race dwelling in subterranean homes, is older than Mr. McRitchie or Sir Walter Scott. In his *Scottish Scenery* (1803), Dr. Cririe suggests that the germ of the Fairy myth is the existence of dispossessed aboriginals dwelling in subterranean houses, in some places called Picts' houses, covered with artificial mounds. The lights seen near the mounds are lights actually carried by the mound-dwellers. Dr. Cririe works out in some detail "this marvellously absurd supposition," as the *Quarterly Review* calls it (vol. lix., p. 280).

Note (e), p. 30.—"Master Greatrake, the Irish Stroaker."

Glanvill, in *Essays on Several Important Subjects* (1675), prints a letter from an Irish Bishop on Greatrex, the "stroker." He cured diseases "by a sanative contagion." According to the Bishop, Greatrex had an impression that he could do "faith-healing," and found that he could, but whether by virtue of some special power or by "the people's fancy," he knew not. He frequently failed, and his patients had relapses. See his own *Account of Strange Cures: in a Letter to Robert Boyle.* London, 1666.

POSTSCRIPT.

It has been said that no trace can be found of a printed *Secret Commonwealth* before 1815. The present editor is inclined to believe that in 1699 the work was still in manuscript. In a letter of Lord Reay's to Mr. Samuel Pepys (Oct. 24, 1699), he says, "I have got a manuscript since I last came to Scotland, whose author, though a parson, after giving a very full account of the Second Sight, defends there being no sin in it. . . . With the first opportunity I shall send you a copy of his books." This description answers very well to Mr. Kirk's treatise, and to no other contemporary work with which I am acquainted, unless it be *A Discourse of the Second Sight*, by the Rev. Mr. John Frazer, minister of Tiree and Coll. There were, doubtless, other parsons busy with these topics; and the minister of Rerrick informs me that several MSS. by Mr. Telfair, author of the tract already quoted, were only dispersed about 1877. Examples of these clerical psychical researchers may be found in C. K. Sharpe's prefatory notice to Law's *Memorials* (Edinburgh, 1818). Such an one is the Rev. Robert Knox, who writes from Cavers to the Rev. Mr. Wyllie on the case of Sir George Maxwell of Pollock. He dare not attribute the mediumship of Janet Douglas "positively to an evil cause. . . . *It is our ignorance of any natural agent* that makes us impute the effects to evil spirits" (*Memorials,* p. lxxv). Moreover, Lord Reay writes as if his "parson" were still alive in 1699, whereas Mr. Kirk "went to his own herd" in 1692. "I am promised the acquaintance of this man, of which I am very covetous." Lord Reay was at Durness, and may not have heard of the mishap which carried the minister of Aberfoyle into Fairyland. It may be added that Dr. Hickes writes to Mr. Pepys about neolithic arrow heads as "a subject of near alliance to that of the Second Sight, and of witchcraft, which is akin to them both." He also speaks of "a very tragical, but authentic story told me by the Duke of Lauderdale, which happened in the family of Sir John Dalrymple, Laird of Stair, and then Lord President. His Grace had no sooner told it me, but my Lord President coming into the room, he desired my Lord to tell it himself, which, altering his countenance, he did with a very melancholick air; but it is so long since that I dare not trust my memory with relating the particulars of it" (June 19, 1700).

Dr. Hickes calls the first Lord Stair "John," Scott calls him "James." There can be no doubt that Dr. Hickes refers to the woful tale of the bride of Lammermoor, who died on September 12, 1669. Law, in his *Memorials*, says she "was harled through the house"—by spirits, he means. This "harling" or tossing about of a patient, probably epileptic, we have noticed in many of the old stories, as in the modern instance of "Mr. H." Now, in his Introduction to the *Bride of Lammermoor*, Scott gives all the authorities at his command: Law, Symson's *Elegie*, and Hamilton of Whitelaw's *Satire*, which avers that Satan seized the bride and "threw the bridegroom from the nuptial bed." Sir Walter was unacquainted with Dr. Hickes' hint, which actually produces the bride's own father as evidence for a story which was plainly regarded as supernatural. It is most unlucky that Dr.

Hickes distrusted his memory.   However, it is
something to feel assured that " a memorable
story" was accepted at the time by the family
of the bride, and was known to Lauderdale.[1]
Lauderdale himself, by the way, was a psychical
researcher, and accommodated Richard Baxter
with some accounts of haunted houses, published
in his *World of Spirits.*   One story of a haunted
house, where a spectral hand appeared, he gives
on the authority of " the Rev. James Sharp,"
afterwards the famous Archbishop.   Lauderdale
inspected the famed Loudun nuns, and saw
only " wanton wenches singing baudy songs in
French."   His letter to Mr. Baxter is dated
March 12, 1659.   His best haunted house is of
the Epworth type.

[1] The letters to Pepys are quoted from his Correspond-
ence, published as Vol. X. of his *Diary* (New York,
1885).